HOMOWNERSHIP

A Gay Friendly Guide to Purchasing and Profiting
from Real Estate and Attaining Self-Reliance and
Financial Security in the Process

by
Mark William Murphy

This book is dedicated to my family and friends who have shared their time and attention to inspire and encourage me, who demonstrated the value of education and hard work, who loved me back to health and happiness.

CONTENTS

FORWARD

While this book was written for the queer folk, you don't have to be, "that way" or "a bit funny" or "on the bus" or "batting for the other team" to read it, learn from it, or enjoy it. Much of the content is true for everyone. It's just that the stories, examples, references, and humor are tilted toward those wearing the lighter loafers. It's written in small, easy going sections, so you can pick it up or put it down whenever you want or need.

There are stories, examples, references, terms and some light humor. I also review some important math formulas to use when deciding (underwriting) a deal. You may want to circle, underline, asterix or highlight info for easy reference later. Make it easy on yourself.

Me: I'll tell you up front, I am not a multi-millionaire with the sir name Kiyosaki, Gates, Wynn or Buffett. I do however have the wealth of experience and insight to share with you my queer family. If along way I help to create more gay millionaires, well, that would be great, fag-tastic, gay-mazing! I do tell you my story, and show you a picture or two to qualify, but rest assured, this book is about you.

You: You know that homeownership is an aspiration many people have. From an early age it is instilled in us as part of the American dream. We were taught that buying a home is as much a part of the pattern of life as courtship, engagement, marriage and raising children. Fine, but what if that's not a pattern you want to follow? Where do you fit in? Is there an American dream for you? Yes there is, and it's time to make it a reality

For those of you who have an interest in home buying but were never taught the basics and benefits of it - who are "buy-curious" but never had the opportunity to follow anyone's example- this book is for you. You all have varying degrees of understanding, but for one reason or another haven't done anything about it.

My goal is to inform and encourage those of you who are still sitting on the fence waiting, wanting or needing something to happen, something to get you going. Read and learn the information in this book. Get a clear sense of the property buying process, why you should buy real estate, and how it will change your life and secure your future. If you don't get what you need in these pages, well, the fence will still be there, but c'mon, let's go.

IT ALL STARTS WITH AN IDEA

You say you want to get ahead, have a little more money, more security? Maybe you feel like you should be farther along than you are. You want to catch up, but you don't know how. The answer is on every city street, alongside every winding country road, borders every body of water. It's real estate! It is property, chattel, the physical, tangible, unmovable holding that has value, importance and security. Real Estate is an asset that you purchase and own, and now's the time the get some. It all starts with an idea. Let's think about it some more.

In order to begin, you should understand the basics and the benefits. That is what's described in these pages. This isn't a book about becoming self- fulfilled, self-realized, or self-actualized. I'm not here to teach you how to solve life's sweet mysteries, how to manifest your hidden greatness, or discover your inner diva. This is not Scientology, Dianetics, or the Kabbalah Center (not that there's anything wrong with that) If you already have any interest in buying real estate, this book will help you, will encourage you, and maybe amuse you too. If you don't have any interest in real estate, I hope to change your mind. It will be one of the best life choices you will make. You will see how achievable and beneficial real estate investing can be.

We gay people are educated, motivated, tenacious and aware. We see the world around us and continue to improve our place in it. In the big picture, we have made significant strides in the pursuit and protection of our civil rights and liberties. Right now, I'm looking at the smaller picture, the individual - you. This book is about helping you. Maybe your improved financial standing will further color the bigger picture, but right now, let's focus on your aspiring self.

SENIOR GAYS HAVE DONE IT

Maybe you know some older gay men and women that seem like they have a few bucks in their pockets. They take exotic vacations. They dress in fine clothes. They drive expensive cars. They have boats and vacation houses. You aspire for those things as well. Good, you should, but you should also know how they got those worldly goods. They took risks, took on more responsibility, and did the grunt work to improve and protect their financial status. They paid attention to the world around them. They took that awareness attribute and directed into the matter of creating their own wealth.

I know these gay men and women too. I also know that they started long before we knew them. They started when they were your age, if not younger. They had jobs. Maybe they were Accountants, Lawyers, Engineers, Nurses or Teachers. They had money coming in but wondered if their job alone would enable them to accomplish their other ambitions. They wanted to go forward, just like you do, so they pressed on.

They invested in property: a small cottage, a house, a condo, a duplex, or apartment building. Maybe they weren't entirely sure of the direction of this property ownership path, but they took action. That in itself was interesting, exciting and motivating to them. It fed their soul, knowing that they took on this challenge and were working to improve their financial lives.

Most of our gay predecessors did not grow up in a comparatively accepting world. They did not openly meet and greet in public, or online. Their activities were private clubs, discreet gay bars, and clandestine encounters.

Homosexuality was thought to be lurid, shameful, a perverse public depravity. There was no openness, no gay liberation, no self-acceptance or civil equality. Those were hard earned on the backs of the gay men and women who cleared our path. Still, despite the discrimination they encountered, they diligently searched and found financing to purchase property. They worked it, improved it, profited from it, until they could afford another and another.

YOU CAN DO IT TOO

The Defense of Marriage Act (DOMA) was enacted in 1996 by President Clinton. It defined marriage as "a legal union between one man and one woman, as husband and wife." It allowed states to refuse to recognize same-sex marriage granted under the laws of other states. It was <u>Section 3</u> of the Act that was its final undoing. It had <u>barred</u> same-sex married couples from being recognized as "spouses" for purposes of federal laws; effectively barring them from receiving federal marriage benefits such as insurance, social security, survivor, immigration, bankruptcy, taxes, financial aid, pension, property, veteran benefits and others. In total, it affected as much as 1,049 laws determining eligibility for federal benefits, rights or privileges. It was met with both acceptance and opposition in varying states. It was litigated up through the court system. On June 26, 2013 it was finally ruled unconstitutional by the Supreme Court, under <u>The Due Process Clause</u> which acts as a safeguard from arbitrary denial of life, liberty or property. Now Gay Marriage has legal protection and due process under federal law.

Gay marriages bring a real financial boost to state and local governments- and they know it. Revenue from gay marriages comes from marriage licenses, higher sales, estate, and income taxes. The "gay dollar" is socially, politically and financially influential. <u>We</u> should "know it." Though we have made significant progress to secure our place in society, we still have a-ways to go. We need to work to improve our individual status first, then collectively, cumulatively improve it societally- even globally.

Walk through the doors of progress that have been opened by our gay predecessors. Make use of what has been so freely given to you- <u>opportunity</u>. Improve your personal potential by attaining financial freedom through timely, intelligent real estate investing.

IT'S YOUR TURN NOW

Take seriously your desire to purchase a property, a home or investment property that you can call your own. As you look around, as you prepare yourself, be aware. Be open to potentialities- both good and bad. For example: Many people associate real estate investing in its current state. They think that because the market is rising, it's a good time to buy. They don't imagine it going down, and if the market <u>does</u> take a down turn, it won't go back up, that it's not a good time to invest in real estate. It's the <u>opposite</u> that is true here. If the market takes a fall- you buy. If your property triples in value- you sell. It's contrary, critical thinking.

My stock broker friend, Big Hugh uses this quaint, simple expression to demonstrate that point, "I buy my straw hats in the fall." Buy it when no one else wants it. Warren Buffett expresses the same sentiment, "Be fearful when others are greedy and greedy when others are fearful."

You are a contrarian, a non-conformist by nature. You already have that self-determined, self-governing, free spirit. You're not like the "other boys" remember? You are an ass bandit, a bootie burglar, a cob knobbler, a dandy, a faggot, a gay, a homo, a joy boy, a limp wrist, a maricon, a nudger, a pansy, a queer, a ring pirate, a sissy, a twister, an uphill gardener, a vine dangler, a wanker, a yanker and a zealot! You've heard it all from A to Z. You've named it. You've claimed it. You own it. It is you, so <u>be</u> you! As that poofy playwright Oscar Wilde wrote "Be yourself. Everyone else is already taken." Wise words indeed Wilde-man.

THE PLAN

I talk about, "the plan", or "our plan" in these pages. I suppose
I could've thrown some sparkle on it and given it a catchier, more
captivating name like: <u>How to Be Financially Free and Fabulous</u>,
or <u>Sugar Daddy Status in Only Four Easy Steps</u> or <u>The Fast and Simple
Secrets to Being Queen of All You Survey</u>. How about, <u>Becoming Your
Own Boss by Investing Your Gay Dollar</u>. Yes, that says it!
Still, "the plan" is what it is, and what we'll call it.

Briefly put here, but expanded on in these pages, our plan is to
purchase distressed real estate - preferably income property at first-
then improve it, gain equity in it, rent it out, then sell it, taking
advantage of tax law, until you can ultimately buy properties for <u>cash</u>.
We'll go through very detailed instruction, insight and examples on
how it's done.

Your life will be enriched by financial success and personal accomplishment.
Notice I didn't say, "financial winnings or gifts." This isn't money you just
acquire for sitting back and doing nothing. You need to be willing to get
involved and do some work.

If you <u>are</u> willing, you will earn a life of financial certainty, stability and
security - and <u>that's</u> worth a great deal - especially as you get old

YOUR MISSION STATEMENT

Before you start hitting the classifieds and the internet looking for property to purchase, you may want to sit down and focus your goal into a Mission Statement. A Mission Statement is a statement of the purpose of a company, organization or person. The Mission Statement should guide the actions of the organization. It provides a path and directs decision making. It can be simple. It can be complex, but both ways spell out the overall goal.

All sorts of organizations have mission statements: Non-profits, Schools, Corporations, Fortune 500 Companies, Departments, Teams, Churches and Community Groups. Why not you?

How are you going to benefit you? Remember, your Mission Statement only applies to you. You can be of service to others later, but now it's all about you, you-you-you.

Here's an example based on this book: "Every day I will consider what I need to do to improve my future through real estate. I will use the newspaper and/or the Internet to expand my thinking and under- stand my options. I will then make a decision and follow through with some action." It's not enough to think about. It's all in the follow through, the footwork.

As you go through this book, I think you will get a clearer view of the actions you need to take, and feel positive and productive as you plan for your future.

MENTOR FATHERS

I always admired my father. He grew up during the depression, fought a World War in the Pacific and overcame his own personal battles.

I remember when I was boy, saying that I was going to write a book on all the smart things he said. It seemed like there was nothing he couldn't do. He was especially handy around the house, and there was a lot of house to handle. My parents owned a 3,500 square foot, six-bedroom Victorian home built in 1880. It was, and still is, on small peninsula of a town called Hull, Massachusetts just four miles across Boston Harbor (pronounced, "hahbah" by we natives).

New England winters can be brutally cold. It's not just the temperature. It's the wind-chill factor. Like any responsible father (of five) my father watched where his money went and tried to control his heating costs whenever possible. It wasn't unusual to see him walking around his house with a caulking gun and putty knife to fill drafty cracks or holes. He also made storm doors and built a wind-breaking fence to stop the freezing winter winds from gusting onto the house.

He did many more odd jobs to the house over the years (that's what father's do) and he encouraged/made all four of his sons help him (again, that's what father's do). Through his mentorship, attention and instruction he demonstrated his ability to problem solve through many home renovation and repair jobs. He also demonstrated his willingness to do the difficult and often dirty work, and he taught his sons to do the same.

My mother wasn't afraid to get a little dirty either, as she was quite adept at completing improvement projects of her own. Now, as a senior, seasoned homeowner herself, she will still occasionally take on an odd job or two. Good for her.

Around that time, when I turned 15, I started taking piano lessons.
I was already performing in school plays and singing in choirs.
The writing was on the wall and it read, "Future Friend of Dorothy's."
I had already cried a year or two earlier when, after watching
The Wizard of Oz, my older brother told me, "Dorothy is dead!"
At that point, it was just a matter of time.

When I was 17 or so, I told my father I wanted to be an Actor.
(another ramp onto the yellow brick road) He said, "Ok, but if that doesn't work out, try something else." I thought that sounded like non-judgmental, reasonable advice (thanks Dad). I didn't know that nearly every other home had their own, "Actor in the family." Nor did I know that nearly every other home had their own budding gay boy. More often than not, they were one in the same person. That's okay. I didn't know what was what until years later, so I went on my merry, gay, little way. I'm sure my father knew that at some point I would snap out of it and pursue something other than acting.

He passed away when I was a teenager. Had he lived longer, I'm sure he would have helped me snap out of it a little sooner, and probably influence some smarter life choices, but, "Man proposes and God discloses," as your grandmother would say.

MENTOR FRIENDS

My late teenage years and well into my late 20's, I abused nicotine, drugs, and alcohol. That was interrupted by a gruelling year recovering from a severe head injury and broken neck sustained in a car accident. After returning to the drugs, alcohol and nicotine for a few more years, I started on another recovery- one for substance abuse.

One would think that with some sobriety, I would be able to pull it together and make things happen. The expression, "Just when things are falling apart, they're really falling together," could not have more inaccurate here. Everything had fallen apart and nothing was falling together. I had no job, no money. I couldn't pay my rent. I was being evicted. I was on food stamps and went to food banks.

My friends often came to my rescue with a meal when I really needed it. They were never short of nourishment or encouragement. We gays take care of our own.

Tax Man Don

I had a friend who occasionally took me to lunch. His name was
Don, or Jewish Don, as he was known back in the 1960's, back in
the pre- Stonewall gay bars of Los Angeles, back when gay men hid
behind the protection of anonymity, even from one another. There
were no names shared then, only identifying pseudonyms like Eddie
the Hat, Motorcycle Mike, Polish Joe and Alabama Bob. They were
all just young, gay drinking compadres, hoping to enjoy a good time
without getting arrested by the police who routinely raided the
place. Don was an older man in his mid 70's when I knew him.
For years he was an Accountant, then started a part time business
as a Tax Preparer, "To keep me out of trouble," he kidded.

One afternoon, over the hamburger special at Frank's Restaurant
in North Hollywood, I was complaining to Don about my troubles,
expressing my disdain about a menial temp job I just got shrink
wrapping commemorative coins. I started talking about how I had
wanted to be a Teacher.

"Why would I want to be a Teacher anyways, where I'd probably only
make $ 35,000 at the most?" I asked with the annoyance of a petulant 7th
grade girl. I indignantly, ignorantly and ungratefully continued my rant,
on and on and on. Don had heard enough. He then took it upon himself to
"take me to school." He looked me dead in the eye from across the table,
and like a verbal right cross he said, "Hey Pal, you're not worth <u>half</u> that!
Who do you think you are huh? You couldn't <u>get</u> that job! You don't have
the skills or the training. You <u>don't</u>! If you want to make something of
yourself, go back to school and become a Teacher, <u>then</u> you can bitch
about it...God!"

That stung. I was hurt. I was embarrassed. There was silence at that table. Don didn't say a word. Maybe he wanted me to really feel the awkwardness of the moment and learn his lesson. I wanted to get up and storm out (again, like that 7th grade girl) but I needed to eat, and in that empty stomach of mine, I felt the truth. Who <u>did</u> I think I was? I couldn't even pay for my own lunch and there I was acting like I was entitled to a six-figure career.

Junk Store John

During those years of financial hardship, I couldn't afford to do much of anything really, but walking was free, so I did a lot of that. One sunny day as I was wandering down Magnolia Blvd, in Burbank, CA., I walked into a thrift store. As soon as I walked in, I was engulfed by heaps of clothing, boxes of books, shelves of knick-knacks and stacks of old furniture. There may have been excessive "thrift" in this store, but there wasn't a person in sight. Maybe the proprietor was buried beneath one of those mountains of used clothing.

As I stood there alone, I noticed a book sitting on a tattered, green vinyl bar stool. On the wall behind the stool, there were a dozen or so black and white photographs of actors and performers. Some of them I recognized, others I did not. I looked down at the book that was placed on the stool. It was a biography of Winston Churchill with a sales receipt from a liquor store being used as a bookmark. I looked again at the piles of debris around me and wondered who would own such a disorderly business, and then I turned in disgust and started to leave through the gauntlet of piled clothing.

Just before I reached the doorway, I heard a deep, resonating voice from the back of the store "Hey Buddy. Hold on," it called. As it walked its way through the narrow aisle of second-hand goods, I turned to see a tall, stout, balding grey-haired man in his early 60's with a wide, grey mustache and large blue eyes. "I had to use the bathroom. Do you see anything you don't need? What can I sell you, you don't want? I'm starting a collection. I gotta raise some beer money for tonight," he said with a smile as he rubbed his hands together. I arrogantly answered, "No-no, I'm fine. I'm just looking around," as I walked the narrow aisle into the store. I didn't want to seem like I was being chased off. "Well, okay then," he agreeably replied. "Feel free to take your time."

I spent a few minutes walking through, looking up and around at all the clutter, then made my way back to the front of the store. The proprietor was seated on his stool reading the Churchill biography. He saw me walking towards him, slipped in that receipt to bookmark his place and said, "You didn't see anything you don't want?" he repeated with light-heartedness. "How about a nice pair of blue jeans? I've got some vintage jeans back there somewhere. Maybe a nice blouse for your wife," he asked invitingly. "I don't have a wife," I retorted. "I'm divorced myself," he admitted. At that point I just wanted to leave. I didn't want to hear this guy's life story, and I certainly didn't want to tell him mine. I impatiently headed for the exit, all full of self and superiority.

"My name is John," he said with a smile as he extended his hand. "And this mess is <u>Sunflower Treasures</u>! What's your name?" he asked. "My name is Mark, I'm an Actor. I just moved here from Boston," I curtly replied, as I grudgingly obliged his handshake. I realized at that moment that this guy would not be easily rebuffed, as he continued to converse with me with questions and light humor. He repeatedly ignored my rudeness. He saw right through me. "Well good to meet you Mark from Boston. Welcome to Burbank! Here..." He reached across the narrow aisle and picked at the mountainous pile of clothing on the table. He pulled out a navy-blue sweatshirt that read "Burbank" on the front. "Here ya go Mark from Boston. This should fit you," as he held it up in front of me. "Now it's official!" he declared, "You are <u>now</u>, "Mark of Burbank!" I half-heartedly protested, "No, no, that's okay. I don't have any money. I can't..." "It's okay," he interrupted. "You can have it."

I became a little nervous, and at the same time stunned by his friendly, generous nature. Though I wanted it, I considered it too nice a gift to give to a stranger. When you have very little, everything is something important. Also, I was embarrassed by my initial attitude toward him, and there he was giving me a gift! "Who is this friendly, generous man?" I thought to myself. "Take it Mark," he insisted. "Next time you come back, maybe I'll see it on you." "You will," I confirmed, and he did. Despite my dismissive disposition, he invited me back. I <u>did</u> go back, and continued to do so for the next fifteen years.

That junk store man became a very important and influential friend to me. He became my real estate mentor. He had already acquired two adjoining houses of his own; one he lived in, the other a rental. Over time he shared his experience, knowledge and encouragement with me. In this little store, he kept himself busy. He socialized with the famous, the near-famous, the wanna-be-famous, and other working entertainment industry customers that crossed the worn threshold of his cluttered thrift store.

Around 6:00 pm, <u>Sunflower Treasures</u> became, <u>The Spit and Slobber Club</u>, as he called it. He and I, and many others over the years, would sit and, "shoot the bull." over a beer or two or ten. Sitting on his stool, surrounded by heaps of clothing, furniture and knick-knacks, John entertained and counselled many a visitor with his wit and wisdom. He also offered sagely advice to those who would take it, and I did, many times.

One evening we were having a drink in his store. I don't recall what we were talking about. I imagine I was sputtering off about not feeling like I was advancing in "my career." I'm sure over the years John got an ear- full of similar whining from other aspiring actors, singers, models and everything else.

At that moment, something stirred in John. His conversational demeanor became more serious, like he just made an important decision- he had. He decided to tell me something very important. He went on to tell me his story of how and why he was able to run his little store without caring if he made any <u>real</u> money. "It's my mad money Marcus," he declared. He continued his important lesson in a slow, deliberate, decisive manner, like he was presenting to me his keys to the kingdom. "Mark get yourself a real job and be careful with how you spend your money. When you have saved up enough money for a down payment, get a loan and buy yourself a house. It doesn't have to be a big, beautiful home, a starter home will due. Get involved in the stock market. When you make yourself some more money, buy yourself some more property, and put a tenant in there to pay your bills." That's what he had done, and he advised me to do the same. He told me months later that he had made an offer on a third house, on the <u>other</u> side of his home, but he didn't want to budge another $5,000. "Someone else got the house and it became a rental," he reported to me. "That lousy $5,000 cost me dearly in loss of sleep, fighting neighbors, yelling children, abandoned cars and other crap. The price was already cheap enough! I don't know what I was thinking. I can be damn stubborn at times. I get that from my mother. She was German."

For years, John had a real job as a Pharmaceutical Salesman. He saved his money to have a decent down payment, then got a loan approved to buy his first house. A few years later, he made enough money in the stock market to afford a respectable down payment and qualified for a loan for the house next door. Between his salary and bonuses, his investments, the rental income on his second house, and a lot of sacrifice, he was able to pay off both houses in less than ten years.

My friend John also advised me to find a parallel career to acting, "I've seen many actors, models, dancers arrive in Burbank with dreams of being stars. Either they run out of stamina or money or both, but they find themselves at the bus terminal with a one-way ticket home. You don't want to spend all your time on the <u>trying</u> and then find yourself at 50 with nothing to show for yourself. Make something of yourself along the way."

Well, it took me almost another year, but I finally landed a job as an 8th grade Catholic School Teacher. I still wasn't qualified, but I took direction and did the work. I made a few mistakes along the way, but still the students learned the curriculum, and that's what mattered. That was my job.

With money coming in from the teaching job, I went back to school. The next year I got into public school teaching on an Emergency Credential. I taught school during the day, while earning my Teaching Credential and Master's Degree in Education at night and weekends. That sounds so easy to state, but really it took me six years to finish both programs. Along the way, I also became a licensed Realtor and started buying and renovating real estate.

MENTORS MISSING

Sometimes, we little gay boys don't get the mentorship, attention and instruction that we want and need. That makes for a few challenging childhood years. As a teacher of Elementary, Middle and High School students, I've seen a number of budding belle boys in my classrooms. I've seen how they get treated and how they give it back, how they fight to fit in and how they falter. Sometimes it's a struggle. (Really, what <u>is</u> wrong with changing a few hairstyles during recess?) They think they're being their own brand of cool, or at least interesting. Along the way I tried to direct them onto a more neutral path, but my input was unwanted for the most part. I was just their Teacher. This was not in my scope of understanding. This was <u>outside</u> the classroom thank you very much. (Oh, ok.) We've known these boys. We've <u>been</u> these boys.

Remember that boy in Jr. High you admired? He was always a bit of a mystery to you. He was an only child. His father died, or was in jail, or took off with his secretary or something. There was some unusual story there, but you never had the nerve to ask him- you couldn't! You only spoke to him once in science lab when he borrowed your scissors to dissect a frog. He always went to the school dances looking really neat, stylish and sparkly. He wore tight, silky, black, bell-bottomed pants, a printed, multi-colored, long sleeved polyester disco shirt, and shiny, black leather platform shoes. There was something different about him, but you didn't know how to describe it. You just knew you liked it, whatever it was. The words "fierce", "fabulous" and "dazzling" were not yet part of your daily vernacular.

He danced every song and had the best moves in <u>The Bump</u>, <u>The Bus Stop</u> and <u>The Hustle</u>. Every step he took on that gymnasium dance floor had the choreographed precision of a Solid Gold Dancer, as moved to the beat of Barry White, The Bee Gees, Donna Summers, Gloria Gaynor, the Pointer Sisters, and The Village People.

"It's fun to stay at the YY-M-C-A. It's fun to stay at that YY-M-C-A-A. They have e-ver-y-thing for you men to enjoy. You can hang out with all the boy, oy,oy,oys". Great! Will <u>he</u> be there? You wanted to be just like him, but you would never admit it. You wanted to dress like him, but you could never, <u>ever</u> ask your parents to buy you such a glamorous, glitzy, groovy outfit - no matter how much you wanted one.

Little gay boys learn early that gay is <u>not</u> okay, so they try to hide it-especially from their fathers- and think they're successful in doing so. They think that their father hasn't caught on yet. After all, he didn't say anything when you wore the guy-liner to the dinner table.
(He was probably ignoring it).

I think it's safe to say, you outed yourself when you showed your family the YouTube video you made of yourself performing Beyoncé's big hit, <u>Single Ladies</u>. "If you liked then you should've put a ring on it. oh-oh <u>Oh</u>, oh-oh <u>Oh</u>, oh-oh <u>Oh</u> oh-oh <u>Oh</u>." Believe me Princess, the secret is out. He knows, and he's not too thrilled about it.

Though he hates to admit it, and maybe he feels a little guilty about it, your father is uncomfortable with who you are becoming. He doesn't know how to handle it. He wants to be there for you, but his inexperience has turned into inattentiveness and estrangement.

Athletic, toned, baseball-playing-straight-sons receive encouragement and admiration from their fathers. Pom-pom-romping, cheer-queer-leading-gay- sons are met with mild praise, and slight embarrassment. They are loved, but not directed, advised or mentored in the same way, so they miss out.

When fathers are talking to their straight sons about getting a good job, finding a nice girl, getting married, buying a house and having children, what's he talking to the gay son about? What station has the cheapest gas and the best place to order a pizza?

Through the years, through meeting other gay men, I've come to understand that not all gays have or had a practical relationship with their parents, especially their fathers. Fortunately, my life brought me other advisers, but it was the mentorship, attention and instruction that I received from <u>own</u> my father that opened the door for these men. I learned the value of following good advice. Thanks to their guidance, I got an education, invested in real estate and arrived at a far more secure and profitable place in my life.

Find yourself a trustworthy, experienced mentor. Mentors have good and bad experiences they can share with you. They know things that you do not. They've done things that you <u>have</u> not. Listen and act on it their advice. Younger gays can benefit from the time, experience and insight that an older mentor can share with you. That's what it's all about.

We older gay men have the "wisdom of the ages" on our side, or so we think. Don't fool yourself. It's always a good idea to seek the counsel of someone more familiar with matters you are not. You know that. Be open to receiving advice.

"When the student is ready, the Teacher will appear," so get ready.

LITTLE BILLY D

The estranged father/gay son dynamic plays out in many families and has been doing so for generations. I've seen it in my own family. My fraternal great grandfather was a busy painting contractor in the early 1900's. His company: Dennehy's Paper and Paste. Mr. Dennehy and his wife had 10 children: 7 daughters and 3 sons. He and two of his sons worked as painters and wallpaper hangers. He went on to purchase a number of residential homes that he rented out, and one large block of buildings. They were mixed-use buildings, having both commercial and residential units. Though all of the properties were eventually sold off, one of those buildings still bears his name, The Dennehy.

Okay nice story, so what? Well, it's not the what, it's the who. Who did not work with his father in the business: the third son, little Billy D. He was the "Nancy boy" of the family, as the Irish call it, though no one ever called it in his family. No one spoke of "such things." Still, little Billy D was treated differently, separately from his brothers.

For lack of mentorship, attention and instruction from his father, he did not learn the value, importance and accomplishment of working, of business. Instead, he devotedly clung to the apron strings of his mother.

His loving, adoring mother was a benevolent contrast to his strict, demanding, dominating father. However hard-hearted he was, Mr. Dennehy was more align with the actual child-rearing practices of the time.

Sigmund Freud's emphasis on Personality Development didn't have any real influence on child development and family practices until well into the 1930's, and by then most families were just trying to survive <u>The Great</u> <u>Depression</u>. So where's a sweet, mild-mannered, piano-playing, poem writing lad to go, but in the safe, embracing, loving arms of his mother.

Billy D didn't move out of his parent's house until his late twenties. He joined the Army Corp of Engineers that went in to help rebuild war-torn Europe after WWII. When he returned home, he spent the next 40+ years of his life as a single man, working as an office clerk and renting the same small studio apartment in Boston. Both his brothers however, grew up, married, raised families, purchased beautiful homes and became leaders in their professions. His older brother became a wealthy building contractor, with business across the greater Boston area. His old<u>est</u> brother became a prominent Boston attorney.

"If it doesn't make a difference, then what's the difference?" is an expression that questions similarity and contrast. Here, the difference is how gay boys are raised. What they are taught. What they miss out on. That very difference <u>makes</u> a difference in how they develop and function as adults in society.

Billy D was a loving, friendly, funny man who dressed meticulously. He was a "Dapper Dan Dresser", he joked of himself. For his own sanity, I hope he dared to step out of the closet occasionally. The gay bars were only a few city blocks from cramped his studio apartment. There was a nice piano bar there too. I imagine him cutting loose and going there to play on occasion, maybe enjoy a Highball or two and a little banter with the boys. Then of course, there was "The Fens", also just down the street. This was an area of tall grassy marshland near Fenway Park that was known for gay cruising and trick turning. Places like that existed for closeted gay men who felt confused, shameful, or fearful, or who were just "revved up" and had nowhere to go.

Maybe you know men like Billy D. Maybe you have an uncle, or an older cousin in the family who never married, who had the same male roommate for years, who bunked in the YMCA for a decade or two. That is how many gay men lived, a life of simplicity and secrecy.

NO MORE RENTING

Today, we no longer have to hide from family, friends, neighbors, co-workers, or the police. We have staked our claim in society and continue to grow in places where we are not. One place we are not is the real estate market. We should own a more substantial share of it. By doing so, we would promote our physical and financial presence in society. Moreover, we would attain self-reliance and financial security for ourselves.

So many gay men prefer to rent, or "lease" as is the more respectable term these days. "I don't rent Darling, I <u>lease</u>, thank you very much." They're leasing everything: apartments, condos, townhouses, cars, boats, furniture, appliances, computer hardware, business machinery, fitness equipment and more. What is this fascination for renting or leasing? Is it more fashionable <u>not</u> to own? Do we feel undeserving, unworthy of owning, of wanting stability? We were never stable before. We never thought of having any of the trappings of normal adult living, because we never thought of ourselves as being normal. You're <u>not</u> normal, so what? You're <u>better</u> than normal! You are your own unique, wonderful self!

Don't be afraid of who you are. Be you! Live you! Love you! The decades of living in quiet desperation are <u>over</u>. You don't have to live at "the Y" anymore, my undercover brother. Enough with the undeserving gay martyr act. That's done, played out, over! You don't have to settle for renting. Settled down in a home that you <u>own</u>!

Ask yourself, what are your needs? Did you miss out on any mentorship, attention and instruction along the way? Do you think you're prepared to move onward and upward? You know you need to improve yourself, but you don't know how or where to start. You have ideas and goals but you're nervous about the process.

Should you be planning and pursuing a business? Should you go back to school for a higher degree or a professional credential? Should pursue that trade career you've always admired?

Don't waste time being confused or apathetic, reckless or clueless. Ask these questions of yourself and begin the process of answering them. Think about it, and then <u>do</u> something about it. Get into <u>action!</u>

COME ON OUT

Acknowledging your needs and accepting the tasks before you is not unlike coming out as a gay man. You thought you could comfortably live a closeted life. "It's no one's business," you thought to yourself. Then you realized, or maybe someone told you, "It's not about them. It's about <u>you</u>. It's about accepting yourself." Once you admitted who you were, new opportunities opened for you.

You started viewing the world with a new pair of glasses (now lavender tinted). You had no idea how much better your life would be once you came out of the closet. You discovered a desire and energy to thrive!

If you haven't come out of the closet yet, that's what you have to look forward to. On the way out, select something nice to wear. You'll want to look nice. <u>We</u> look fabulous.

So hey, make sure you're giving yourself a clean shot at opportunity here. Help yourself dissolve those doubts, those phantom feelings of failure. Feelings aren't fact. You'll reach your potential when nothing is holding you back. Get out of your own way and move straight ahead, rather, gayly forward.

I QUALIFY

For many of you the status quo is enough. You don't have to settle for "enough," when you can have <u>more</u> than enough. You can be like those older gay men and women who cruise around the world taking exotic vacations, who have money, property and security. The time to start is now!

"Buy real estate, and take care of it, and it will take care of you."
My friend and mentor taught me that expression, and I've found it to be true. It has served me very well so far. My real estate investments have paid for two duplexes, four houses, a condo, six own your owns, two mobile homes, graduate school, my cars, my boat, and several exciting trips around the world.

My first piece of income property was purchased in 1997. It was a big old barn of a duplex, up the driveway, behind its garage. I lived in the downstairs unit and rented out the upstairs apartment to a gay friend of mine. Wanting to maximize the income potential of this property, I turned this duplex into triplex by converting the garage into a clean, dry, liveable unit. I suspected it wasn't legal, but I did it anyway.

Now cities are less strict on garage conversions due to lack of housing. Only <u>now</u> it would be called an <u>Accessory Dwelling Unit,</u> an ADU. If you have a large enough yard, you can even buy prefab, prebuilt ADU and rent <u>it</u> out.

(**Side note**: If you're going to do a remodel, repair or rebuild project on your property, don't make a big show of it. You don't want gawking eyes on your tools and materials, or city inspectors looking for permit violations)

My first duplex...

and its garage, with a younger me, ready to start the clean-up.

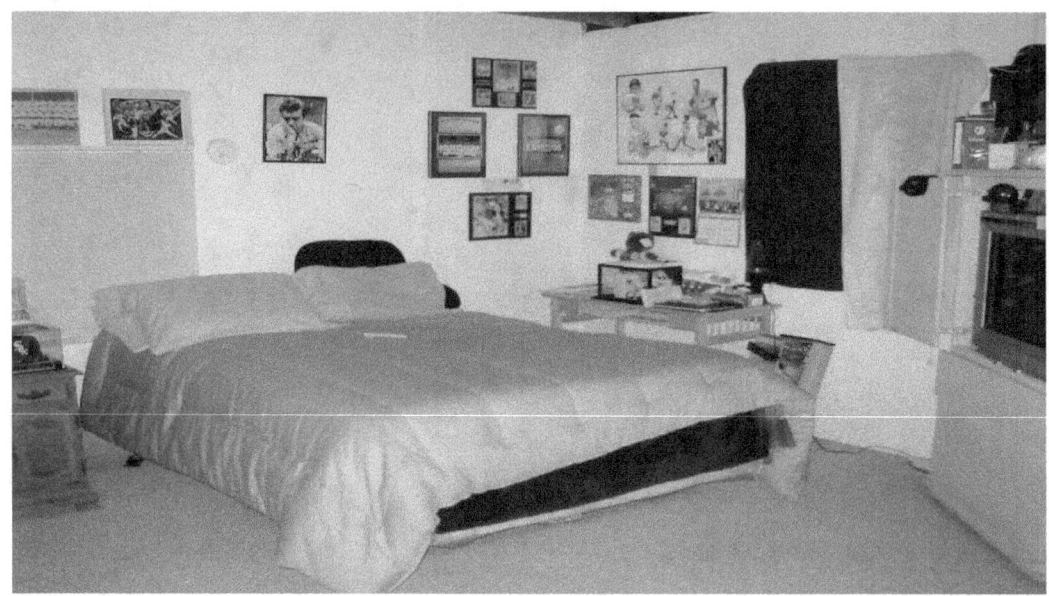

The garage, now "Guest House" all renovated and rented,

with running water, toilet, double sink and shower stall.

I used 2x10 planks to elevate the bathroom floor to enable the water from the drains to flow downward.

Toilet drain pipes. It has to go somewhere. Under it all, it's just wood and plastic.

I dug a long ditch, and then laid some pipe to connect the guesthouse drainpipes to the duplex's drainpipes, which flowed into the city sewer line. This was for the plumber to do. He cut into a section of the sewer pipe (the bottom diagonal one) then added a connector pipe, then attached the drainpipe from the garage bathroom to the connector pipe, 1,2,3. The top of the pipe stayed at ground level. It was the <u>clean out</u>, which provided access to the pipes if it ever needed to be rootered/drilled clean. Most houses have clean outs. They're often painted over, but they're there.

I explain this job and show it, because I want you to see that even though some projects may seem difficult, they are not. It's a matter of putting the pieces together. The hardest part of <u>this</u> project was digging to find the sewer line.

The guesthouse unit also had to have water and gas piped in. Clearly this is also the plumber's job to do, unless you have your own pipe bender and blow torch (you butch thing). Pipes can be placed almost anywhere. You just have to clear a space for them. On the previous page you see that the pipes were positioned under cement walkways.

Let these pictures be an example of how projects like these get done. They may be of some encouragement when you start your own projects.

When the new guesthouse was completed, I found a very nice, handsome and friendly gay guy to rent it.

With the income from the upstairs unit, and the income from the ex-garage now guesthouse, all my bills were being paid. The positive cash flow allowed me to save my income from my teaching position. It also allowed me to qualify for a loan to <u>buy the house next door,</u> which I purchased in 1999.

I also followed my mentor's additional advice and became involved in the stock market. I made enough money for the down payment on that house and the porch that I built on the front of it.

This is a picture of the duplex behind the garage, now guesthouse unit, and the house next door. I was not a fan of the original lime green color of the second house, so I painted them both burgundy.   It was here that I discovered that I was a Lattice Queen. Can you tell? Wait, it gets worse.

Kitchens and bathrooms are the most important rooms in a house, and the house next door needed a complete kitchen remodel. I took my trusty heavy-duty sledgehammer and started furiously swinging, slinging and demolishing the old countertop. (On the next page you'll see the before and after pics)

In the demo process

Nice and new.

As soon as the last brush of paint was applied, I found a nice lesbian couple to rent the house. They were together a few months and decided to shack up. They moved in, and five months later, they moved out.

I got a gay male couple after them. They didn't stay too long either. They wanted to live in an area with more nightlife. If you want an exciting, exhilarating, electrifying environment, don't move to Burbank boys. Try West Hollywood, or "WeHo," as the locals call it. WeHo, where the young, sexy and stylish reign "Supreme," with Diana Ross realness.

After the boys moved in, then out, I got another tenant right away. He was a worldly, older, gay gentleman. "Auntie" worked as a Jeweler during the day and enjoyed coming home to a quiet neighborhood at night. Perfect for Burbank! "Burbank, where old people go, to visit their parents."

With a gay man on top of me, (upstairs apt) a gay man front of me (the guest house) and a gay man next to me (as a tenant/neighbor) what more could I do, except put a gay man behind me, and convert Auntie's garage into another liveable guest house. Here a queer, there a queer, everywhere a queer-queer.

I also wanted to add to the usefulness and value of the property for when I would sell it. I knew an additional unit on the property would do just that, and it did, and does significantly.

I converted Auntie's old garage into a lovely little Guest House, with lattice accent of course.

All sides of this old corroded, termite-ridden garage were solely and entirely deconstructed and rebuilt by yours truly. Where there's a will there's a gay. I mean way.

Rebuilding the side: new studs, new plywood, new paint (and more lattice)

Rebuilding the side (Where's Shaggy?) and primed to paint.

Put in a new/used window, paint and even more lattice accent.
(Where's Shaggy?)

The inside had to be reinforced, insulated, dry-walled and painted to become another clean, dry, liveable unit...

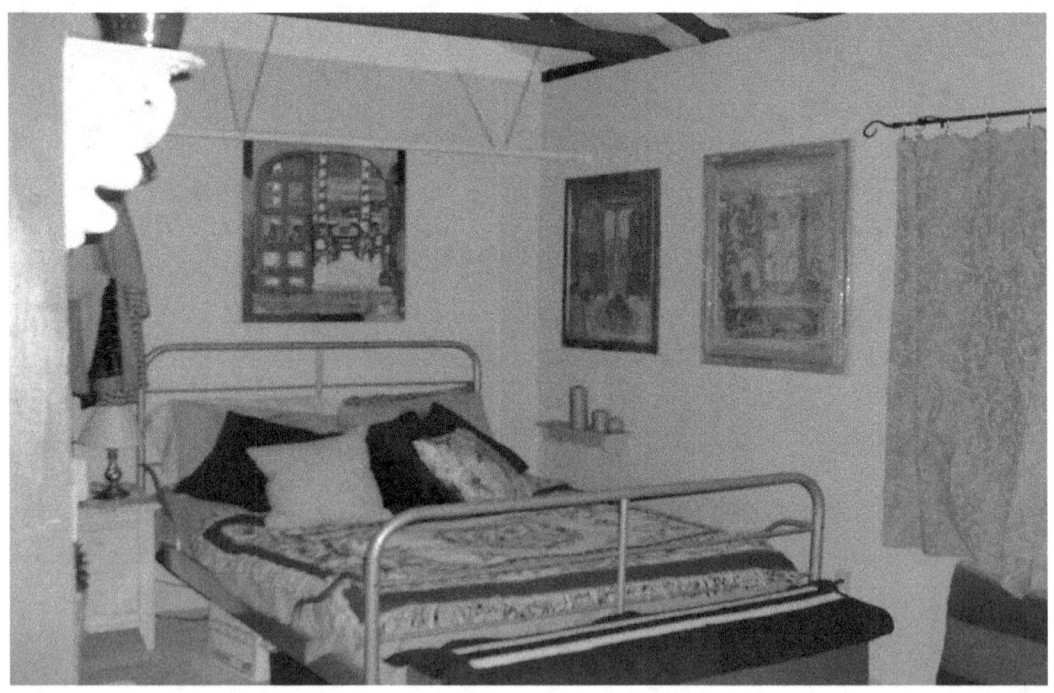

which it did.

Complete with a kitchen...

and bathroom (still in the works here)

4306

4308

2301 - I'm like Shaggy. I have to leave my mark wherever I go. Woof!

You could call it, "paying attention," "being nosey," or "being a Mrs. Kravitz," but in 2004 I noticed my neighbor started showing his own house and guest house to people, to well-dressed people, to professional type people. I also noticed him inviting other neighbors onto his large corner lot. Well! I became very curious. I put a scarf over my pink foam curlers, wiped away my cucumber face cream, put on my fuzzy slippers and flannel housecoat, and scurried over to find out what was going on. It was as I suspected! He was poking around for a buyer for his property. Really! And he never even asked me! So what if he didn't know me yet? How dare he leave me out!

I stifled my disgust over being deprived of this opportunity and presented myself to him. I expressed my sincerest, earnest interest in his property. I had already owned the two houses next door. I thought his two houses should be mine as well. I was the "heir apparent." I thought if I pictured it and pursued it, I could make it happen. Someone had to buy it. Why not me? Why not you?

The Seller and I became friendly over a couple of cheap cigars and even cheaper meals. The only trouble in this new-found friendship was that he made a handful of homophobic comments that I didn't care for but, whatever. I had a house to buy from this boob. I wasn't about to change his red-necky ways. That's his problem.

Pick your battles boys. Harvey Milk you're not.

I thought his asking price was fair enough, knowing that they both needed some work. I used a Home Equity line of Credit for my down payment. I managed to qualify for my third mortgage and bought it - bought them.

I had the other two properties rented, so I moved into this house, and made the necessary repairs and improvements.

I had every intention on renting them out to more Gentlemisses at some point. I was going to be a Burbank Land Baron(ess) but the real estate market was good, too good to wait. I sold them, paid off all of my bills and the mortgage on my second house. While buying is nice, owning free and clear is nicer. That's our plan's goal.

I was able to buy two more houses on my street than my mentor John did on his. "The student surpassed the master," he admitted proudly. "Good, that's how it's supposed to be."

Here are some Before and After pictures of that property.

The two houses on the <u>other</u> side of the duplex.

Painted in and out, some new flooring, updated bathrooms, and a few plants here and there, and of course it had to be enclosed by lattice- of course.

Eech! Paint much? The house in back, not so nice.

The Garage Door: Deconstructed, strengthened with 2x4's, tarpaper, insulation and plastic.

It was to become an additional living space, so it had to stay warm and dry. It was both.

With a rebuilt garage door, a few nails, a paint job, and lattice accent, this little house was almost ready to be occupied.

This side still needed work. (Where's Shaggy?)

Nothing some fresh paint, a turf lawn and a homemade lattice fence couldn't cure.

Put it all together and whattaya have? "Murphyland!"
My own little gayborhood. The gayest block in Burbank.

It may not be worthy of Design Star. I mean HGTV will not be calling anytime soon, (although I invite that handsome Scott McGillivray to call me anytime). Still, I had managed to purchase half the block, 14,000 square feet, three contiguous lots, four houses, a total of seven units, all on a teacher's salary and other people's money. Hmmm, maybe Scott should call me. I could be like his older, long-lost Irish uncle, who joins the show whenever Scott needs some Income Property advice. (Snap out of it Erin Go Braless. That's not gonna happen).

Fortunately, the property further increased in value thanks to the capital improvements of the city of Burbank. On my street, right in front of my house, they replaced the obsolete, abandoned, railway tracks, that were lined by old, dry, raggedy shrubs, with a new, spacious, landscaped bike path. It was a nice improvement to the street and a welcomed addition to the community.

Grubby and shrubby, with rail tracks already removed.

Getting prepped

for this new community bike path.

After the recession of 2000, real estate was climbing out of a low pricing period. It reached its peak during "the housing bubble" of 2005-2006. The Economist magazine wrote, "The worldwide rise in house prices is the biggest bubble in history." I saw that it was great time to sell again, so I sold the house I had moved into, my second house. I took the profit, paid off and moved back into, my remaining duplex.

When the real estate bubble burst in 2007, values plummeted, and prices followed. This resulted in many owners holding, "negative equity," where their mortgage debt was higher than the current value of the property, what we now commonly refer to as being, "upside down," or "under water."

Though the financial forecast was bleak, the National Association of Realtors saw a little sunshine rising in home prices in the last two quarters of 2008. Though this sounded favorable, it wasn't. There was little supply and even less demand for housing. No one was buying. Here's where you step in, or in this case, me.

In 2009, when prices were low, I purchased another duplex that I moved into. I repaired and improved and eventually sold it, making a sizeable profit on it. Why? It's not because I got lucky, though I am Irish. It's not because I'm the smartest guy in the class, the sharpest knife in the drawer, or the brightest crayon in the box (pink of course). Believe me, I am not. It's because I entered and exited the real estate market at the most opportune times. You need to do that also. That's the plan man.

If you want to get into the market, acknowledge that and get into action. Start by getting your financial house in order.

"There are those who watch things happen. There are those who make things happen, and then there are those who wonder <u>what</u> happened." Who do <u>you</u> want to be?

You can do more than just watch your friends and family buy property for themselves. You can buy one <u>yourself</u>, then you won't have to wonder what happened to all of your money over the years. Once invested in real estate, you will have the benefit of watching it grow in value, in a property that you care for, in a property that you <u>own</u>.

PREPARATION

In real estate, <u>Success Comes When Preparation Meets Opportunity</u>.
The best way for a Buyer to be successful, is to be prepared with a Pre Approved Loan, then both sides of the deal will <u>know</u>, that you will have the money to purchase the property you are pursuing. There will be no doubt or question or worry. The funds will be there – great.

When you present your Offer, <u>with</u> your Loan-Pre-Approval Letter,
you're also showing the Seller that you are serious, that you're not there to waste their time or to, "play real estate" but that you are there to <u>buy</u>. They will appreciate that – your preparation. It will give them a sense of security in the deal and a confidence in you.

You want the Seller to like you, to favor you, to favor your prepared/<u>preapproved</u> offer, and not just for their acceptance (you want that) but also for their indulgence
(you may <u>need</u> that)

For example, if you <u>are</u> in escrow, and there's a problem - some delay or dispute - your good favor with them, will earn you their good <u>will</u>, if you need extra time from them to <u>solve</u> that problem.

Many times deals get made, not by the terms (price, condition or credits) but by <u>timing</u>; who is quickest at the draw, who has the money hand, ready to buy. Show them that you have the money and are motivated to make it a quick, short escrow.

Time can also be the enemy, the saboteur, and can kill a deal. People change their minds, terms and conditions change, vendors have to reschedule, paperwork get unsigned. Offers and approvals expire. Don't let it linger. Keep it moving. Get it closed.

Preparation pays, in a number of ways. Being prepared is being smart, or
as Emerson put it, "<u>The future belongs, to those who prepare for it</u>."

Take that as advice! Prepare for your future with a pre approved real estate loan, so **<u>you</u>** will be successful when your preparation, meets **your** opportunity.

Sure it's important to aspire and admire the things we desire. We all want and hope for goodness in our lives. That's only the starting point. Wanting and hoping are not strategies for success. We are not going to base our future on luck. We have to take it to the next level. We need to focus on our aspirations and start planning for their achievement.

Our goal is to achieve financial security through real estate. You need to start the process of preparation, and that includes your down payment.

You need to start holding on to your money, even if it's only a little at a time. There's no such thing as extra money, short money or chump change, not if you have financial goals. Put aside that idea and start putting money aside as well. Start collecting that "extra money," that "chump change" into a glass jar and watch it accumulate in size and value.

Consistently, and faithfully save with every pay check. You don't have to spend every dollar you make. It's okay to live a little below your means, so that you have more money to save. You're starting on a plan to buy real estate. The first part of that plan is saving for a down payment.

THE HOME BUYING PROCESS

It's a good idea for you to see what the Real Estate Buying process looks like.

1. Hire an Agent

As you are the Buyer, your agent is called, the Buyer's Agent. (clever huh?) A Buyer's Agent will represent only you and has a fiduciary, a trusting responsibility, to look out for your best interests. Buyer's Agents may ask you to sign a Buyer's Broker Agreement, which simply states that he represents you as the buyer. Do that. It's no big deal. You're not married to him. You're just going steady for a while, and you can break up at any time. Really, it shows that you're serious about your agency relationship and that you won't cheat on him.

If you are the Seller, your agent is called, the Seller's Agent, or more commonly, the Listing Agent, because they are the ones listing the property for sale. They have a fiduciary responsibility to you to negotiate the deal and do the paperwork on your behalf. Usually, it is the Seller who pays the commissions. In reality, the commission money is coming from the money the Buyer going to pay to purchase the property, but on paper, the Seller pays the commissions to both the Listing/Selling Agent and the Buyer's Agent.

2. Get prequalified, then preapproved

Order a free credit report online, or have your Lender do it, and fix any mistakes on it. Ask your Agent for a referral to a Mortgage Broker but look around yourself too. Maybe you have a friend, or family member who is hooked up with a Lender. Maybe there's someone at your bank that you're friendly with or <u>want</u> to be friendly with.

There is that exquisite, exotic, caramel colored customer service stud Ricardo at your credit union. Hmmm, your gay-dar detects his presence, position, direction and distance as <u>soon</u> as you enter his office. You've always wanted to talk to him too. Go over and start chatting him up for a loan. He'll give you a Rate Sheet with all the info on it. Take it for later, because you <u>know</u> you're not going to remember a damn thing he says. Between his thick, wavy, jet-black hair, his brilliant beguiling smile and his muscular, broad shoulders, you are reduced to a mumbling, muttering mess...silly you.

After you pull yourself together, compare the rates offered by your bank and/or credit union, with other lenders. Visit and bookmark Bankrate.com. It has a variety of info on rates, fees, retirement, taxes, insurance and much more.

Rest assured, finding Mortgage Broker will <u>not</u> be difficult. They'll be glad to see your handsome, home-buying, loan-hungry self, walking down their aisle. Who knows? Maybe you and Ricardo will also.

You will soon be asked to supply your financial information and proof of any assets. Now would be a good time to create a file on yourself. Keep copies of all the important financial documents: check stubs, W-2's, tax returns, rental agreements, bank and investments accounts if you have them. You will need to submit all of these documents when you apply for a loan.

I assure you, this will make the application process easier when you have all your info together. You will feel well-prepared. Also, this may not be the only loan you end up applying for, so get it all together.

Further into the process, after the Lender/Underwriter has examined your application, supporting documents, verified your income and ran your credit report - you are preapproved! You have a solid figure that you know you can borrow.

Determine your maximum loan amount, but only choose a mortgage type that you understand, with a monthly repayment amount you know you can handle. It may well be less than the maximum for which you are approved. You don't have to take it <u>all</u> just because they're willing to loan it to you. You still have to pay it back, so take it easy. Don't be greedy- be measured. Ask the Lender to give a Loan Approval Letter. It is your "Proof of Funds," showing that you have the money, and that you are a legitimate buyer. This separates the (serious) men from the (lookey loo) boys. Having that letter in your hot, house-hungry hands will give you the knowledge and security you need to find you an affordable, suitable property.

3. Look at Homes for Sale

For a moment, forget about your Pre-Approval amount, and think about what you need and what you want in a real estate purchase. Where you want to live is a good start. Do you want a condo or cabin, townhouse or triplex, split-level or raised ranch? How many bedrooms do you need? How many bathrooms? Maybe you have some valuable vintage vehicles that need garage protection, or will on-street parking for your moped be enough? Is a gourmet kitchen an, "absolute must" for those formal, fanciful, black tie affairs you throw? Maybe you're just an Ellie May /Paula Deen country gal at heart and would find a big ole vittle-fixin' country kitchen better for when you, Enus and Anus are hankerin' for some of Granny's Baked Stuffed Possum and Lima Bean Tater Gruel.

What about a Jacuzzi and/or a pool? That sounds interesting! It would be nice to have a place to cool down on those hot days and nights. Maybe you want to host some summer extravaganzas! If times get tough, you can always charge admission and start your very own backyard bathhouse.

Maybe, just maybe, you want to take off some pounds, and a low impact, stress free, aerobic form of exercise like swimming would be a suitable activity for you. Have you considered a cement pond, a pool? (Pool boy not included). Also, you may want to think about a yard. How large of a yard? Large enough to practice your chip shot or putting?

So get your thoughts together gays, guys, girls. Decide what you want and need in your real estate purchase. This way you spend less time looking at an inventory of houses that don't fit your needs, and more time thinking about the nuances that each house has to offer. Think about it, do you really need a wine cellar? You just want the cellar (I'll say no more on that).

4. Write a Purchase Offer

Now that you have selected a property, and have your finances in order, and after considering a number of important factors (i.e., what the financial potential of the property is) you instruct your Agent to put pen to paper and write your Residential Purchase Agreement- your offer.

5. Negotiate and Write Counter Offer

Expect the Seller to issue a Counter Offer, unless you're paying the full asking price. Sometimes a Counter Offer is not over price, but over closing costs, or the condition of the property. If you have timed it per our plan, the house is priced in accordance with its fixer condition or low market value. Don't waste your energy or theirs "dickering over the piddly." Translation: Don't be a pain in the ass over little things. Compromise and come to an agreement. If it's the price you're stuck on, remember you're buying this property to ultimately sell. You can make the up the difference at the other end. After you improve it, you profit when you sell it. Don't be "penny-wise and pound foolish", just get the deal done before it slips away or someone else steps in.

6. Make an Earnest Money Deposit

Accompanying your Offer goes your deposit. While no deposit is required in order to make a contract binding, it is a show of good faith, of sincere intent, of "Earnest Money Deposit." Without the money, you're not a real buyer. You're just playing real estate. The more you put down, the better your offer will look to the Seller, especially if there are competing Buyers. Your Agent will tell you who to write the deposit check to. It could be to his company's name or an escrow company. Do not make it out to him, definitely not to the seller, and of course, never _ever_ give anyone a blank check- no matter how young and cute he is- _especially_ if he's young and cute (sorry twinks) Lastly, the check has to be good. It's going to get cashed and held in escrow as soon as your offer is accepted and escrow is opened. If you bounce a check here, then it's over from the start, and all you did was waste people's time. People can waste their _own_ time. They don't need _you_ doing it for them. Make sure your check is good, and you're good to go. If you need help with raising a deposit, speak to a Realtor. There are programs available that you can apply and qualify for. Stick with it.

7. Open Escrow / Order Title

Your Agent or Transaction Coordinator (T.C.) will open Escrow and Title, if the Listing Agent hasn't already done so. The T.C. will take the lead here, and make sure this transaction is handled correctly and timely. Ask for the Escrow Officer's name, phone and escrow file number. Give this information to your Lender and your Insurance Agent. The T.C. will keep everyone on the same page.

What is Escrow? "Escrow" is a strange little word. It comes from the French word, "escroue", meaning a scrap of paper or a roll of parchment, which indicated the deed that a third party held until a transaction was completed. In real estate parlance, "Escrow" refers to a third party in a transaction whose job it is to hold all the funds and pay obligations such as property taxes and insurance premiums for the borrower. One of the last functions of escrow is to "convey Title", or transfer ownership to you. We think that Titles bestow special rights, importance and honor. We think of The Duchess of York (Fergie) King of the Jungle (Tarzan) Mistress of the Dark (Elvira) and of course, the very Queen of the Desert herself (Pricilla).

8. Order Appraisal

An appraisal is the market value of the real estate-the house and land combined. The bank needs to see this appraisal to be sure the property is worth what they are willing to loan you to buy it.

9. Comply With Lender Requirements

Lenders may ask for additional information prior to closing, like a cancelled check to show that a certain payment or bill has been made.

Word to the Wise: Do not change your financial situation while in escrow. Do not go out and finance that red Ferrari convertible you've had your eye on, or put another gay cruise on your credit card, or finance an expensive computer system. Keep everything the same. Changing your indebtedness will definitely change- if not cancel- your loan qualification. Also, don't change jobs from one company to another company. An interoffice promotion won't cause a problem. Changing to another company entirely may, so stay put, at least until loan approval.

If you have a Daddy Warbucks in the wings and he decides to give you substantial sum of moola for services rendered- keep it a safe place. Your underwear drawer is not a safe place. A home safe, a lock box, a safety deposit box is. Do not deposit it into your bank account. Sure, it's an additional asset that will be come in handy later on, but now that you have already applied for a loan and are in the process of being approved, the Lender/Underwriter (the person who will decide your financial fate here) will see it as odd when he asks for your most recent bank statement. He's going to question: "Where did you suddenly get this money? Why didn't you report this money before? Are you reducing the loan amount you are applying for? Who is this tall bald man in the tuxedo? Will he adopt me too? I do have that curly red wig at home." (Well, maybe just the first three).

Just keep this additional money to yourself, wherever it comes from. If you didn't report it at the beginning of this process, don't report it now. If it turns out you don't qualify for the loan and you reapply later, <u>then</u> you can show it as an additional asset. That's when you can account for it. It's fine that it's a gift. You will just have to write a letter explaining it as so. Don't feel you have to write <u>why</u> he's gifting it to you, or what you did to <u>earn</u> it. Keep it on the "D.L.," the "Down low." Some things are better left unsaid.

When your Loan Application File is complete, the Lender will submit it to the Underwriter for final approval. They will analyze the risk to the Lender and reserve the right to ask for additional conditions to be performed before they, "fund the loan" or give you the money. This is where a sudden burst of credit spending, or sudden appearance of new money in the bank could kill the deal. Don't apply for new credit or give your personal information to anyone who might run your credit. Additional credit inquiries may hurt your credit score and will have to be explained to the Underwriter. Just sit tight and wait for loan approval

A TIP: If you start getting cold feet about buying the house, don't get your knickers in a twist, or your panties in a bunch and quit the deal. Talk to someone: your sister, your brother, your mother, your therapist. It will pass. You'll be fine.

10. Approve Seller Disclosures

The Seller must inform you, must <u>disclose</u> to you, the condition of the property, any defects or malfunctions or material facts that you need to know. For example, if the property is in an Earth Quake Fault Zone, or a Wildfire Area, or if the appliances are known to be defective, the Seller must provide a disclosure to let you know. Your Agent and Transaction Coordinator will get you the disclosures. It's then your job to review 'em, approve 'em, sign 'em and return 'em.

11. Order Homeowner's Insurance Policy

It's a good idea to start shopping for a homeowner policy as soon as your purchase offer is accepted. You're not going to close escrow until you have it, so call your Insurance Agent right away. If you don't have an Insurance Agent, get a referral from someone you trust- maybe you best gal pal. She'll know one. She's got her affairs in order, always has. Give her a call.

12. Conduct Home Inspection

Hire a reputable Home Inspector. He or she will review the entire house, from the foundation to the chimney. A comprehensive report will be written, reviewed with you, and then and given to you.

13. Issue Request for Repair

If the home inspection discloses health and safety issues, your Agent will issue a Request for Repair, by asking the Seller to address (or repair) those issues or give you monetary credit for them. You can have them repaired on your own later. Getting credit for repairs is another way of getting the price reduced, even after you've reached an agreement. As long as there is an unresolved request for repairs, there is an issue, and the deal is still negotiable.

Another Word to the Wise:

Some Buyers see this Request for Repairs as the one last opportunity to try to squeeze some money out of the Seller before the deal is done. My advice: don't do that. Realize no home is perfect, and the Inspector may find faults. Be reasonable about their severity. Also, the plan is to get the house cheap, so you're already getting a good deal. What did I say before? Don't dicker over piddly things. If you want a new bidet, buy one yourself or...use the sink.

14. Weasel Clause

In California, you have up to 17 days to remove contingencies. In other words, as a homebuyer your offer is contingent upon the fulfillment of certain conditions you write into the contract. If any of the contingencies are not fulfilled, according to the terms in the Residential Purchase Agreement, you can back out of buying the home and take your good faith deposit with you. In by gone years, Real Estate Agents used to call contingencies, "weasel clauses", because a contingency would let Buyers cancel, or weasel out of a contract without the penalty of losing his earnest money deposit.   A few examples of contingencies are: Appraisal, Loan, Home Inspection, Lead Paint, Roof or Sewer Inspection. If any of those conditions don't go the way you want, you can back out. For our purposes, just remove them and go forward. Remember, you're buying a fixer.

15. Do Final Walk-Through

Do not pass this up. Though you're not buying a pristine palace, you should inspect the house. Make sure it's in the same condition as when you agreed to buy it. Check the kitchen and bathrooms. Make sure they didn't take that gold-plated toilet bowl throne that you looked forward to taking your daily constitutional on. If you find any serious or unexpected issues, address them then, before you close escrow. "It's now or never."

16. Sign Loan / Escrow Documents

You will sign escrow documents shortly after opening escrow. You will agree to pay the terms and fees of your loan. This needs to be done at the start, so everyone is in agreement, and you know what you're taking on. Of course, further into our plan you will be buying for cash, so <u>no</u> loan docs will be necessary.

17. Deposit Funds

It used to be that <u>you</u> were responsible for depositing the funds, for bringing a certified check payable to escrow. You would be like some Fortune 500 corporate rainmaker whose presence and influence yielded successful business transactions. Now, not only do they <u>not</u> need you, but they don't <u>want</u> you. They just assume spit on you as to look in your direction. They don't want to count on <u>you</u> to stand your sorry, swishing self in line at the bank, to pick up a check to bring to them. These ladies are doin' it for themselves. Now it's all highly coordinated and communicated. Between emails, texting, voice mail, electronic signature websites and applications, you are person-non-gratta. Your Transaction Coordinator is in touch with your Title Rep, and is in touch with your Escrow Officer, who's also in touch with your Lender. Everyone is touching - touching - touching. They're like a well-oiled, dare I say <u>lubed</u>, machine. They don't need <u>you</u> there Mr. Fancy Pants, obstructing their efficient flow. "Just step back Bum Chum! We've got this!"

18. Close Escrow

This is the last step here, and it's a good one. Here the documents get filed in the County Recorder's Office. The Property Deed, which is the legal instrument that shows that the Title on the property was conveyed to you, was recorded, filed. "Mr. Gay Sexy Fabulous, a single man", is now the owner of record. Mazel Tov! Your Deed of Trust, which is a legal notice that documents your loan, if you have one, is also recorded with the county. It is the security for your loan. If you don't pay the loan, they <u>will</u> come after you. Remember, they know where you live.

Sometime in the future, when you sell this home, this investment, you will want to receive what's called a <u>Deed of Reconveyance</u> from the County Recorder's office. It is the legal instrument that states that the Seller, you, have paid in full the mortgage associated with that property. This means you're free and clear of the debt on that property. Time to move on to the next one.

MAKING A BUCK

As with any money-making enterprise, you are starting a business here, and you should treat it accordingly. Your business plan is to buy low, improve it, gain equity, rent it out and/or sell it and move on to the next one. You will do this one, two or more times. Along the way, you make a nice profit on the monthly rent. You'll do your best to create a quality product (your property) that you sell for, a significant profit, so that you can eventually buy another property for cash. When you buy for cash, the rent is <u>all</u> profit. It is all cash flow and becomes a very secure source of income. That's the objective. You're doing this for the money. What business operates for anything else? "It's not greed. It's self-interest", said Economist, Milton Friedman. It's Capitalism. There, I said it: Capitalism, Money, Profit!

You may be thinking, "But hey, we're gay (and not for pay). We're not about money. We're about social equality, justice, fairness!" Yes, we are for all those things and more, but we can also be about making a buck. It takes money to advance our political and social agendas. It takes money to advance ourselves. Money is not the root of all-evil. Don't be afraid of success. Don't be embarrassed by it. Don't feel guilty about it. Don't apologize for it. When you have attained it, you will have <u>earned</u> it.

Capitalism keeps the wheels moving. It's the great motivator. It's what keep us working to improve our lives. It's the American Dream! Start living your dream. Get moving on improving your life. You've been wanting to do something. Time is going to go by with or without you. Make good use of it. Don't waste it on delusions of grandeur, or fear of failure. You're only a failure if you give up. So, c'mon! Get involved! Get to work.

THE NOT- SO GREAT RECESSION

The 2007–2012 global financial crisis, also known as
The Great Recession, The Long Recession, and The Lesser Depression
is considered by many economists to be the worst financial crisis since
The Great Depression of the 1930s.

After the Dot Com bubble burst that caused the Stock Market Crash
of 2000 and the economic slowdown that followed, Federal Reserve
eased credit availability and drove interest rates down to lows not seen
in many decades. Banks loosened their lending practices. This lead to a
credit boom that fed global speculation in real estate. This manic,
almost panic drive to purchase real estate reinforced the risky lending
practices.

People were allowed to take on mortgages with ridiculously easy terms:
Interest Only, No Down Payment, No Income Verification, No
Employment Verification, No Appraisal, Cut or Uncut, Top or Bottom,
Straight or Gay.

Money was easy to get and there was trouble in the streets. "Oh we got
trouble, right here in River City, with a capital T that rhymes with P
that's stands for pool." Ahhhhh will the big Broadway Baby in the
back quit singing show tunes? We're talking money here. Thank you!

Anyway, these easy to qualify for loans were called, "Sub Prime."
To first understand Subprime, you must know what Prime is. The
Prime Rate is the interest rate that commercial banks charge their most
creditworthy borrowers. If you're not a credit worthy borrower, you are
considered subprime. Consequently, you present more of a risk to
lenders, so you pay higher interest rate.

It sounds contradictory. If you are subprime (or under prime) you should pay less than, but no, you pay <u>more</u>. If you are less-than you pay more-than. (How rude! You are <u>never</u> "less-than" Dandy man).

Subprime borrowers are often turned away from traditional lenders because of their low credit rating (often below 600) or other factors that suggest that they have a reasonable chance of defaulting on the debt repayment. Well that's exactly what happened, and in very large numbers. It's what triggered, <u>The Great Recession</u>.

The failure of these subprime mortgages was the first symptom of the credit boom to bust, and the following real estate collapse. Low quality mortgages further fuelled the financial fire (too much alliteration?) Also contributory was the transfer of assets from the balance sheets of banks to other financial markets. These were called Mortgage Backed Securities, (MBS) which were shares of loans that were processed and packaged, sliced and diced, bundled and bought by larger banks that sold them to other lenders.

It sounds harmless enough. "Money begets money" is the old Amway slogan. It's also an excellent and safe way to make money when the housing market is booming. In the early 2000's the U.S. housing market was booming. A person who bought a new home in January 1996 for $155,000 could reasonably (easily) expect to make a profit of $100,000 when selling it in August 2006, but 2008 wasn't 2006. 2008 saw nothing but Subprime Mortgage Default, one after another after another.

The problem was, people stopped paying on these risky mortgages. Mortgage holders defaulted, causing the banks to default, but now at much higher levels of debt. The MBS that were sold and resold and resold were now worthless. It became a disastrous domino effect of default (more alliteration abuse). Add to that was the complete failure of rating agencies, bank regulators and federal supervisors to detect and correct this man-made-monetary-monsoon (ok, that's enough).

The Federal Reserve too, did nothing but encourage the wild west of lending. It wasn't until the middle of 2007 that the Fed decided it was time to rein in the abusive practices in the subprime lending market. That was like closing the barn door after the horses were gone.

The housing market collapse and bank failures resulted in evictions, foreclosures and extended unemployment. The crisis caused the failure of key businesses, losses to consumer wealth estimated to be in the trillions, and a downturn in economic activity leading to the 2008-2012 global recession.

SIGNS, SIGNS, EVERYWHERE THERE'S SIGNS

If you were paying attention to the housing market news during the Global Recession of 2008-2012, you heard many stories about the number of houses being foreclosed. You saw and heard words like, "foreclosure", "short sale" "bank owned", "distressed", "default" from the television, radio, and newspaper. You felt sympathy for the poor slob who had to vacate his house in that miserable economy, and you were glad you didn't own a house. You thought you were smart for staying away from all that. You thought you were getting off easy. You didn't have to manage the taxes or insurance, or the upkeep of real estate. Besides, you were young, or young at heart, and gay. You didn't have a wife and kids to support. Your only responsibility was you. You had your apartment, a nice car, maybe a 401K for good measure, and you thought you were looking good. That was enough for you. Great! Well, first off, everyone looks good in their 20's and 30's. We're young, fit, attractive and wanted. Love that, love yourself, love others, really that's a wonderful time. You can be all those things, and at the same time, look ahead.

Now you should be asking yourself, "What can I do to continue this goodness into my 40's, 50's 60's and beyond?" If you're already a mid- career man or a retiree (and still as enchanting as ever) you can improve the financial status of your retirement years. Pad that retirement mattress with money made from real estate. 401 K plans, while good investments, may not satisfy your needs when retirement comes around. Who knows when the government will start looking at 401K contributions as taxable income? Invest in your future. Invest in yourself. Invest in real estate and you will achieve financial independence.

SHORT SALES

You've heard the threatening, worrying word, "Foreclosure" before. You know nothing good comes of it. What about "Short Sale?" That doesn't sound so bad. Well, it's not entirely bad for the seller, and it's potentially good for a buyer.

A short sale is when the lender (the bank) accepts a discount on a mortgage to avoid a possible foreclosure auction or bankruptcy. In a short sale, the property sells for less than, or "short" of the balance owed on its mortgage. The property can be a house, an apartment building, or even vacant land.

In a short sale, the property owner has arranged with their mortgage lender, to accept a price that is less than the amount they owe on the property. As part of this deal, the lender agrees to forgive the rest of the loan. As a result, the seller is released of this debt and doesn't have to go through the foreclosure process, which would be even more damaging to their credit score.

The lender avoids the burden of having to unload the property for a potentially huge loss, and some lucky buyer picks up a property for a discounted price. It's easier all the way around, though not entirely equitable to the lender, still it gets the job done.

Banks grant short sales for two reasons: the seller has a hardship, and the seller owes more on the mortgage than the home is worth. Not all short sales requests are approved. The bank will rarely approve a short sale unless the borrower is seriously behind in their payments.

A few examples of a hardship are: unemployment, reduced income, divorce, medical emergency, bankruptcy and death. Overwhelming Botox bills and lack of storage space for your Jimmy Choos and other shoes does not qualify as a hardship- though I feel your pain.

If you owe more on your mortgage than the property is worth, then you are, "under water," That would qualify as a hardship. In some of these cases the mortgage holder, the owner, may want to cut their losses and get out. They apply for a, "Strategic Short Sale." This is when the seller could <u>probably</u> afford the payments, but for some reason doesn't want to, so they don't.

Maybe the neighborhood has gone downhill and feels unsafe to them. Maybe a freeway is being built in earshot of the property that disrupts their Chi. Maybe they're uncomfortable about the new business opening down the street called <u>The Naked Man</u>. Little do they know it's just some queer clothier with a risqué sense of humor. Whatever their reason, they want out. That's too bad for them but potentially <u>good</u> for you. Maybe you can pick up this house, this duplex, this building, this commercial lot for a significantly reduced price.

When you <u>buy</u> a short sale property you are not buying it from the owner/seller but directly from the lender/seller- the bank.

For example: A homeowner, who is facing foreclosure, has an existing first mortgage of $300,000. You write an offer to the lender for $220,000, which is accepted as full payment for the loan. Your immediate equity is $80,000. Think how long it would take you earn eighty thousand dollars! Suddenly you find yourself sitting on a strong and sizeable wad (of money) all because you were prepared, attentive and active in your pursuit of buying real estate. <u>That's</u> how it's done.

FORECLOSURE

The process of taking possession of a mortgaged property as a result of someone's failure to keep up mortgage payments is called Foreclosure.

If you stop paying your mortgage and the bank won't approve your short sale request, the next exit is Foreclosure Road. That is a route you <u>never</u> want to take. The road to foreclosure is a long one. The same reasons that cause short sales can also be the cause of foreclosures: medical conditions, loss of employment, divorce, etc.

The very word, "foreclosure" puts fear and panic in the hearts of every property owner. We picture an evil, unfeeling, merciless Banker banging at the door. Dressed in a dark black suit, a tall black hat and black handlebar mustache, he orders the occupants to immediately vacate the home they love so dearly. It's a crying shame we know. We can just see that cute little house, enclosed by a white picket fence, that's owned by a widowed mother who fell on hard times. That heart-wrenching dramatic scenario, while compelling, is generally very unlikely. There is time recover. There <u>is</u> time to make good on a defaulted loan.

The foreclosure process is not difficult to understand. There are several stages during which the homeowner has an opportunity to bring the loan current and avoid foreclosure.

The first step your lender takes is to file a <u>Notice of Default</u> with your County Recorder's office. The NOD allows you, the public and any junior lien holders (like that contractor you never paid) to be notified of the default. You have a reinstatement period of 90 days from the filing of the NOD to bring your loan current or the foreclosure process continues.

If you can't come up with the money, you still have another 20 days after the lender files a <u>Notice of Sale</u>. After being sent to you via certified mail, a NOS will be posted on your front door or gate, and on some spot near your house (usually a telephone poll). It will also be published in your local newspaper. (Consider your dirty laundry aired). The NOS must be filed at your County Recorder's office at least 14 days before the sale. As you can see, there are definitely time parameters that must be followed, which gives you time to stop the foreclosure process and save your home.

If foreclosure is unavoidable and the property must be sold, it is done so at a <u>Foreclosure Trustee Sale/Auction</u>, which typically occurs on the steps of the County Courthouse of where the property is located. The time and location of the sale are designated in the Notice of Sale. At the Trustee Sale, the property is auctioned in public to the highest bidder, who must pay the high bid price in cash, typically with a deposit (of $5,000) up front and the remainder within 24 hours.

Many of these properties are already worth less than the total amount owed to the bank, so the bank is willing to hold on to them. They become "REO" or <u>Real Estate Owned, aka, Bank Owned</u>. They will then go back on the market at the discretion of the lender, the bank.

Now when you're looking for a property to buy, you will have some indication of what some of these properties have been through. The history of these properties could, and should, influence what the seller is asking and what you're willing to pay. Be mindful of the signs.

PLAYING REAL ESTATE

Some of you are already playing real estate. You're renting a house or a condo. You have a <u>sense</u> of ownership. You have fixed it up just the way you like it. You have all the comforts of home. The landlord is great. He doesn't mind what you do to the house, what colors you want to paint the rooms, or how you fix up the backyard. He wants you comfortable, content. He wants you to feel at home.

That sounds all warm and fuzzy doesn't it? There may even be a lint ball of truth there, but really, the landlord wants to get you in and keep you there. If letting you paint the bedroom magenta with black stripes is going to keep you there for a year or more, it's no loss to him. If you're happy, he's happy. As an experienced landlord myself, I know. It only takes a gallon or two of paint to change it back to something less... fabulous.

Guest House/Granny Flats/Garage Apt Living

Maybe you're renting someone's granny flat, a guesthouse, or a converted garage from a friend, or family member. You practically own it. It's not very spacious, but you make due. Sometimes you get a break on your rent if you work around the property, or you watch the landlord's kids.

In this "practically owned property", you have access to the backyard most of the time. You can use the pool most of the time. The landlord doesn't mind you having people over most of the time, as long as you, "keep it down". He has however, been quite pointed about this: No public displays of affection!! "No gay PDA. You can keep all that sort of stuff inside the walls of your rental." Really? Is that why you get up for work every day and put in long hours, just to pay your rent to some inhospitable homophobe? It shouldn't be and doesn't <u>have</u> to be.

I know when you're younger you really don't mind putting up with some resistance, but while you're giving in, being compliant to your landlord, time is going by. You get older, maybe a bit more mature, maybe a bit less obsequious. You realize you want to live freely, without interference. If you already have a few more years under your belt, you may be thinking, "Why the hell am I putting up with this?" It's certainly not too late to change your living arrangement.

Control your <u>own</u> environment! Don't spend your valuable time and money living in someone else's. You are in charge of who and what comes on your property when you own it, govern it, control it.

Timesharing

Lastly, there is the favored, fashionable, fanciful frolic of the timeshare experience. It seems like a great way to pretend you own property without actually owning it.

A timeshare is a different kind of real estate purchase. Instead of paying full price for the property and owning it yourself, you pay a share of the price, which allows you to use the property for a certain period of time every year. That time period can be a fixed time, or a floating period of time within the year.

Most timeshare purchases are Deeded Timeshares. This means that you, the purchaser, are buying an actual share of ownership in the resort. Non- Deeded Timeshares, also known as Right-to-Use, Certificate or Vacation- Interval timeshares, are more like a club membership. You have the right to use the property for a specific time period but don't actually own any real property.

Timeshares are not investments in real estate. It's more like prepaying your vacation hotel for the next twenty years. Better to put your money into an investment and let the investment's profit pay your hotel bill.

Once you purchase a timeshare. You are locked in. You can't sell it. You can't give it away. You are stuck with ever-increasing maintenance fees and special assessments on a property that you no longer want.

In short: Don't do it. Buy your <u>own</u> property. Pay your <u>own</u> mortgage, not some developers.

YOU GIT'

I would not have written this in 2001 to the tail end of 2006, when property values increased exponentially and money was cheap and easy to come by. People bought property that was grossly overpriced. Lenders gave loans to people who could not afford them. Cheap money lead to the gross inflation of property values. People who had homes that suddenly became so (too) valuable, used them as their private banks. They took out Home Equity Lines of Credit and borrowed against the value, albeit over inflated value, of their home.

In 2005, I saw my neighbor's little-nothing-of-a-house sell for $520,000. I stood across the street from my houses looking at them and thought, "I should sell. Now's the time." I'm not a Banker, or an Economist. I was just paying attention. It was simple math really: addition and subtraction. I considered a possible sale price, minus what I owed on the house.

With the profit, I paid off the mortgage on house number 1- the duplex. I was also able to pay off my home equity line of credit, my credit cards, and even walk away with a significant amount of money that I later invested in another duplex. That's how over-priced houses were, and that's why I got out when the "gittin was good," he wrote with rancher realness. I suggest you do the same. Take your profit and move on. Though those houses are worth much more now, so is the money I made on them and reinvested.

I was able to make more money selling in the high, because I spent less money buying in the low. I wouldn't say prices are low today, neither are mortgage rates, but it's important to get into the market, to have a position. I got my first 30-year mortgage at 7.375% which allowed me to buy the duplex that I later leveraged to buy more and more properties in the years that followed.

DUPLEXES/INCOME PROPERTY

Other people's money, or O.P.M: Three letters that will help you get to where you want to be. It's the cornerstone to capitalism. Other people's money can make it happen. As I previously wrote, my first property was a duplex. The rental income from the other unit helped me pay for and improve the property. The additional income can help you qualify for the loan on a property you otherwise wouldn't. Rental income can pay the mortgage, and the taxes, and quite possible the utility bills. Of course, with all properties, you don't want to pay a high price. Remember, you want to "steal it". If you can't steal it, you don't want it. How much of a steal is the variable, but that's what you want to do. In this market, rental values are comparatively high. If you find a duplex "on the cheap" - grab it. Again, the rents can carry the note if not other bills as well. Now, the money you earn at your job can pay for whatever else the rental income doesn't cover, as well as improvements, or "Capital Improvements", which again, are improvements or restorations that improve the overall value or increase the useful life of a property. Capital Improvements can be made by you, as an individual homeowner, or by your municipality.

Say you build a deck on the back of your house. (Your brother gave you a hammer and a circular saw to butchen you up). Is that a capital improvement? Sure is! You make a coy pond in your backyard. Is that a capital improvement? No, just an aesthetic one- enjoy it.

Now, what if your local municipality builds a new public park near your house? That's a capital improvement to the town, as well as to your property. A park in your area adds value to your home. "And that's a good thing," as Martha Stewart would say.

BE A WORK HORSE NOT A SHOW HORSE

After you find yourself a suitable "fixer property" with financial potential, the work to repair it, to improve it begins. The fixer generally needs a lot of upgrading, both inside and out. If you're willing to do the work, you will find yourself performing these tasks, though not necessarily in this order: attaching, adjusting, anchoring, bonding, unclogging, cleaning, cutting, capping, coating, cementing, demolishing, digging, dusting, dismantling, filling, fastening, gluing, hanging, hammering, installing, joining, nailing, patching, priming, painting, raking, replacing, reattaching, repairing, restoring, sticking, sweeping, scraping, sanding, sealing, shortening, tightening, lubricating, mounting, caulking, screwing, and wiping (spanking is discretionary). Some of these tasks will fall well within your gay skill set (certainly the last five) others will not. No doubt there will be a bit of a learning curve, but you'll soon straighten out, get the hang of it.

Also, get yourself a Home Depot, or Lowes, or some other hardware store credit card. You're going to need it. Tell your friends and family that you would like to receive tools (yes tools) as holiday and birthday gifts. You're definitely going to need those too. If you really want to surprise them, ask for a cordless, multi-headed, oscillating, reciprocating power saw. They're not going to know who you are anymore.

While there are number of things that you can't do, there are many things you can and need to do. Resign yourself to getting dirty. Real estate investing is not always pretty, but well worth the elbow grease. You can be a show horse when you're done. Now you must be a workhorse! So put on that harness you've been saving for Leather Daddy Night and get to work.

GET A GUY

Now, there are Guys, and there are Guy's Guys, and then there are Guy's Guy's Guys. (Stay with me on this) Your brother in law is a Guy. When he needs something done that he that can't or won't do, he calls <u>his</u> Guy. If the Guy's Guy can't do it, then he calls <u>his</u> Guy, which then becomes, the Guy's Guy's Guy. Get it Guy? I mean Gurl-Guy?

Even though you are being a workhorse, there will still be tasks you can't or won't do. Young or old, first time buyer or seasoned owner, there will definitely be a job or two that you won't want to do. It is here you call the Gay Guy's Guy. If the Gay Guy's Guy can't do it, he will call <u>his</u> Guy, who will then be the Gay Guy's Guy's Guy. Anything beyond that, they're pretty much a stranger, like a second cousin twice removed.

Once you get your property, start cruising around for a Guy. He won't be on some gay website, or hanging out on some street corner, or in some park downtown. You will find him in the local paper. Look for ads that say, "Handyman Available", "Maintenance Technician", "Residential Contractor", "Husband for Hire", "To-Do List Doer". They're out there, and they're looking for work. I'm sure you could find one on Craigslist. One day when you're bored and you're tired of trolling Casual Encounters and Men Seeking Men, you should slide on over to Jobs. It is there you will find your man, your Guy, your Gay Guy's Guy.

When you do find one, let him know what your plans are for the property. Tell him that if it goes well, you will use him frequently and faithfully. Tell him you're, "looking for a guy", just keep your hand off his knee.

THE WORLD'S GREATEST LANDLORD

BEING A LANDLORD AND A PROPERTY MANAGER

Whether you purchase a cottage or a condo, a triplex or town-house, a building or an abode, you're going to have to maintain it, manage it and protect it. If you, "Hold Title" to a property you are The Lessor, The Landlord, The Aristocrat, The Land Barron, The Supreme Master who rules over all he surveys (Ahhh-no). You can try to play the part of the Feudal Roman Nobleman who dispenses protection and justice among his dependent peasants with a wave of his sword, but really, that's not how it shakes out, no matter good you look in your gladiator garb. Don't think Russell Crowe. Think more in terms of say, Mr. Green Jeans. Less heavy metal, more farmer overalls, to handle the numerous odd jobs that property ownership demands. You are its subject, its slave, for the first year or two anyway. Worry not. You'll be victorious in the end.

If you oversee the renting of this property, or a part of it, you are now a Property Manager. Congratulations! If it's a single-family house, a duplex, a triplex, a multi-unit or mixed-use building, whatever, it will need your attention - so will your tenants. This is what you will do to earn an income. It's not that difficult. You put in a little face time on the property. You take care of an odd job every now and then. You keep it rented and collect the rental income each month. There are a lot harder ways to make money.

For those of you who are quick to proclaim, "No! Nay! Never! I will never be a manager of property," as if it were the most repulsive, wretched, despicable, detestable, disgusting job to perform, I say, "Fear not oh Jockey of the Sausage, oh Admiral of the Rear, oh Player of the Piccolo, oh Pirate of the Ring (one more) oh Tosser of the Salad. It is well within your ability." If not, forget it, and pay someone else to do it.

"Do what you can do, and pay for what you can't or won't," my Mentor taught me. You don't have to do it all, if you don't want to. There are people you can call to get the job done. You can work on the next project.

If you are the property manager, there's only one thing you have to be concerned about: everything. You are in charge of conducting all business- related duties involved with your rental properties: renting, tenant screening, collecting the rents, paying the bills and taxes, maintaining and marketing the property to keep it fully rented and evicting when necessary.

Of course to avoid eviction, you should always try to resolve any conflicts. You've got to be a little flexible if the tenant is having problems. If they don't have the rent, give them time, and see how it develops.

If their money problems start becoming your money problems then you've got a problem (yes I wrote that). You should consider a Three-Day Notice to Pay Rent or Quit. It may be time for them to leave. However, would kicking them out and having a vacant unit for an unknown amount of time become a hardship for you? Maybe you should work out some type of arrangement, like a week-to-week payment plan until their finances become more stable. Some money coming in during is better than possibly no money after, the month is over. Plus, a payment plan would keep the tenant actively involved, or "on task," (as Teachers like say) in meeting their rent obligation. It's certainly not what you expected or wanted when you rented to this tenant, but people do experience financial problems- most of us have.

A TIP

Even though are rightfully upset at your tenant for the financial distress they are causing you, try not to be righteously indignant. Getting angry with them over your perceived sense of "injustice," is not real. It's nothing personal. It is what it is. They don't have the money. Restrain your tongue from "telling them off" and your pen from writing them a, "You're a selfish bastard," letter.

It may feel good to do. It may make you feel superior to them, but really, it will just come back to bite you. So you take the high road, before your tenant takes the low road, and takes a hammer to your toilet or pours concrete down your drains. "Restraint of tongue and pen," will serve you well every time.

PROPERTY MANAGEMENT SERVICES

If you invest in an income producing, but you don't want to manage it yourself, you do have the option of hiring a management company to do it for you.

You may be unable, uninterested, unwilling or unskilled to perform the numerous functions of property management. There are certain times to manage your own properties, and then there are times when it makes more sense to hire someone to do it for you.

If you have a triplex that's 10 hours away from you, clearly you can't be running over there whenever there's a problem. Even if those problems are few and far between, you need a manager that is physically close to your property. They are there to be attentive to your tenants and to the building when necessary, usually with a team of maintenance men (with plumber's crack).

It may be that your property is just down the street from where you live, but you just don't want to manage it anymore. Maybe you are an older gay man who lives a relaxed life of retirement and travel and you don't have the interest. Maybe you have multiple properties and you don't have the ability. Maybe you have another full-time job and you don't have the time. All that is perfectly reasonable.

You may have one, two or more of these properties that are paid off. The money coming in is all passive income, all cash flow. It's well-worth the nominal monthly fee the management company will charge to allow you to pursue your other interests: tennis, golf, water polo, nude yoga, whatever.

You will find that once your tenants are settled in, the properties will not be a constant concern, whether you get a property manager or not. Provided your properties are in good condition, and that you have rented to decent, responsible people, they'll be no back and forth. Most tenants want to be left alone, just like you do. You know?

HOW TO HOLD TITLE, YOUR ROYAL FAGGOTRY

"Holding Title," gives you special rights, importance and honor in a property. It proves that you are the current, rightful owner: lock, stock and barrel. It proves that no individual or government entity has any claim, lease, lien, right or restriction to or on your property. Once your Title is transferred, or "conveyed" to you, you become the King of your Castle, the Princess of your Property, the Empress of your Environment, the Duchess of your Domain. (Tiara not included).

Now, land is as old as time itself. Through the centuries, a parcel of property may change hands dozens of times. At any point along the chain of ownership, problems could arise that cast a "cloud" over a title, putting a claim of ownership in doubt. To make sure there is no cloud on your title, Title Insurance companies are in business to make sure your rights and interests in the property are clear. They issue Title Insurance Policies to guarantee that fact, for as long as you own the property, all for a modest one-time premium when you buy the property.

Title Insurance companies extensively search relevant public records to determine if anyone other than you has an interest in the property. They'll be no surprises.

You don't want any former owners (like that Amish family) long lost relatives (like your drunken cousin Liam who just got out of rehab) or old boyfriends (like that young, handsome, soap opera actor who bunked there for a month) knocking on your door claiming ownership to your property. A Title Report and Title Insurance will prevent any and all of that from happening. You can sleep easy. Your arse will be covered-for once.

When a Title is conveyed, or transferred, it must be put in someone's name. That is called "Vesting" (sounds so monastic). <u>How</u> it is specifically vested is of primary importance. The name on the Title of your real property can control how your property passes when you die, how much tax your survivors will have to pay, and how freely you can manage your property while you are alive. Also, if it can be financed, improved or used as collateral. This is particularly important to you as a real estate investor, who may very well refinance it, or use the equity as collateral in a Home Equity Line of Credit. The most common of these methods of Holding Title are as follows:

Joint Tenancy: Owned by at least two people, where all tenants have an equal right to the account's assets and all have survivorship rights in the event of the death of another tenant.

Tenants in Common: The way two or more tenants own a property. If one owner dies, the other does not automatically take the entire estate. It is transferred to the descendant's beneficiary.

Tenants by Entirety: The way hetero married couples hold the title to a property. One spouse can't modify his or her interest in the property in any way, without the consent of both spouses. When one spouse passes away, the surviving spouse gains full ownership of the property.

Sole Ownership: Simply, the Title is held in one person's name- yours. It will read as so: <u>Mr. Gay Sexy Fabulous, a Single Man</u>. You may want to leave it to someone in a will, in case you pass away early but, you're probably not going to have it that long because you bought it as an investment (you decide).

Community Property: Held by a husband and wife during their marriage that they intend to own together, either spouse has the right to dispose of one half of the property or will it to someone else.

Community Property With The Right Of Survivorship

Community property with the right of survivorship is a way for married couples or Domestic Partners to hold title to property (the Gay way). If one partner passes away, the other gets ownership of the Title.

THE NEW GUY

Remember when you were young, drunk and oblivious, and did things you would never consider doing now? You went to places where you thought you'd never "socialize," never mind the people you <u>slept</u> with that you wouldn't even have <u>lunch</u> with today. Remember those days? Well that can still happen, even when you're <u>sober</u>!

You may find yourself a distressed property that's in a lower income neighborhood, in an area you wouldn't be caught dead in, on a street made for drunks, drug dealers and vandals- or so you think. Sure, you may occasionally smell the scent of marijuana wafting through the air. Maybe you'll periodically have to pick up some empty cans of beer, shot bottles and fast food wrappers from the front of your house. It's okay. Don't be nervous. Put your balls on dear. Man up gurl. Muster up the nerve, the huevos, the gonads, and get to work. That's why you're there.

You're the new guy on the street. Let people see you improving your house, thereby improving their neighborhood. When you see a police car driving by, give a friendly, acknowledging wave hello. Let them know who you are. Show them you are now part of the neighborhood. They'll be glad you're there when they see you're remodeling that rundown eyesore of a house. You may even see your neighbors start working on their own houses. You are encouraging to them, and they like it.

One afternoon you turn onto your street, and you notice that your neighbor has erected a white flagpole with Old Glory flying atop, waving in the wind. He nods and smiles at you as you drive by. They have become comfortable with you, and start greeting you, praising your property improvements. "Hello Sir, how you doin' today?" "Have a blessed day now alright?" "You got that place lookin' good!"

You learn that the neighbors don't like the beer drinking, pot smoking, littering loiterers either. You realize that they're really very pleasant people. They send their kids off to school every day and put in a full day's work themselves.

You start to feel proud that your efforts have made such a positive impact on your street. It would seem that you have put the "neighbor" back in the "hood." Where you were once thought of a stranger, you are now seen as an approachable, friendly fellow, and that feels nice.

THE HAUNTED HOUSE ON THE CORNER

In a two-story corner building, covered with three shades of gray, graffiti-marred walls, broken windows, a weather beaten front door, a shabby, rotted garage door, a set of urine-stenched stairs and a litter-lawn for a yard, I found my next investment; a neglected, distressed, art-deco duplex…my new home.

No one had lived in it for four years. My first day there some neighborhood kids came over to meet my dog Shaggy. They kept asking me questions, interviewing me, being curious kids. They told me that the house was haunted. "Good, maybe that will keep the kids away," thought this crabby old man.

The kids didn't stay away for too long though. I had a large yard and my sociable Shaggy dog that they often wanted to play with. That only lasted a short time though. I soon got a city permit, and put up a tall wooden fence, 8' high by 30' long, "to keep the dog in the yard", I told the kids. I knew if I started yelling, "Hey you damned kids get the hell outta my yard!" amiable acceptance would not come easily.

More than one neighbor suggested I put up an iron barred fence, instead of the tall wooden fence that I painted white. "They're gonna tag you. That's what happens around here." Maybe so I thought. My new fence was like one long, tall white board, begging to be tagged, but I didn't care. I wanted to protect the dog and have some privacy. (You know how we are about our privacy).

Well, I <u>did</u> get tagged, twice over two years, but it was easy enough to paint over it and still well worth the trouble. Iron Barred Fence, please. Where am I, Alcatraz?

As I fixed up the house, making those capital improvements, I was building equity, as well as improving the neighborhood. Now it's the nicest house on the block.

That renovated property not only improved the look and appeal of that neighborhood, but also the values of the properties in it. The investment of time, energy and money proved to be well-worth the effort, for me and for everyone else on the block.

The next page has some before and after pictures of the property as it was being renovated.

THE HOUSE ACROSS STREET

While my Art Deco Duplex is now in very good condition and has great curb appeal, the neighbor's house is an eye sore, and always has been. It's the worst house on the block and presents a very disturbing impression to potential buyers of my own property. This is the house that they would have to look at every day.

I can't ask the neighbors to clean up their property. They were foreclosed on last month. Now no one lives there. It's just going to sit there abandoned, dilapidated, lifeless until it gets sold off. Who knows how long that will take? "I can't let it hurt the potential sale of my own property," I thought to myself. "What do I do? What can I do?" … Did someone say, lattice it? Sure! Why not? I strapped some lattice onto their beaten, battered, twisted chain link fence to hide as much of that pathetic property as possible. Lattice is cheap enough, and covers a lot of sins. At least I won't dread a negative reaction when buyers see that house, or fear it being the cause of my own house not selling. It changed the look of this neglected property, to a normal, cleaner looking one. No one's going to complain about that.

Sometimes you have to take the initiative to fix what no one else will, to pick up trash in the street, to discard abandoned furniture. You may not be the only one who cares about the potholes on the street, but you may be the only one who is willing to call the city. Go ahead and call them and continue to call them if they don't show up. That's their job, and they need to keep working too.

Clearly, if they don't know about the potholes, they can't repair them. Make that part of your job to tell them. It's okay if you take charge. Someone has to. You're already operating on a different current. You're gay!

Neglected next door, in need of a facade lift.

How about a lattice lift? Sure! Why not?

WHO YOU AINT'

After some time and some saving, you qualify for a loan. You find yourself a fixer upper with some rental and equity potential. The owner just wants out, and sells it to you, "as - is" for a low market price. Great! That's it- just what you want! The neighborhood isn't really what you're used to, but hey, you're willing to put in the time and do the work. That's how the <u>plan</u> works.

In this new neighborhood, there are a few bold, outspoken, dominant women. They are the mothers in the neighborhood. They are your new allies. They keep it all in working order. These ladies are large and in charge of the happenings in this hood. Don't fight it. They know what they're doing. They keep their eyes and ears open to what's going on, especially when it comes to their kids, or anyone else's for that matter.

One afternoon I was pulling weeds and cutting the crab grass in front of my duplex, and a group of teenagers were hanging out on the opposite corner exploding "F Bombs" all over the street. Out from a neighboring window came a loud, reprimanding voice, "Who's that I hear cursin' like that? Is that the way your <u>Mama</u> taught you to talk? I don't <u>think</u> so. <u>Get</u> yourself away from my door before I call her down here to drag your trash-talkin' self home! Go on!" (The kids mutter to themselves) "What's <u>that</u>? Don't you <u>make</u> me come down there! I won't <u>wait</u> for your Mama!"

The kids all looked at each other, then scattered like frightened birds. I kept on working but had a good laugh over it. For a moment, I imagined getting a scolding of my own. "And <u>you</u>, Mr. New Neighborman! It's about <u>time</u> you cut those weeds, and <u>when</u> are you gonna paint over that graffiti and <u>fix</u> those broken windows? Don't you <u>make</u> me have to ask you again!" Yes Ma'am!

Even though you have purchased this property like a grown up big boy, you hold Title to this lot of land, and you have staked your claim on the block, this is <u>their</u> turf. You are a stranger to them. You are an unknown, unproven, and as yet unwanted quantity. You have no "street cred", no power over anyone. My advice: don't be in a hurry to get any. You won't need it.

Also, no matter how authentic and authoritative she is, no matter how much you want to show her off, you've <u>got</u> to restrain your inner, "Sassy black woman." Yes, that's right. Leave-her-be. Don't play that part here. It won't work. It's not going to hurl you to the top of the neighborhood hierarchy, no matter how good your head-bob is. It's not going to help you fit in. It will only be seen as a mockery of these mothers, however unintentional. You don't want to undermine them. It's not neighborly or wise. Don't try it on the adults or the kids. Even the little girls have part down. They learn it early too.

One late afternoon, after having just returned from a jog, I took a seat on my bottom front step, before ascending to my apartment to clean up and have dinner. My street was especially quiet, and there was a cool breeze blowing, so I thought I'd take a moment to rest and enjoy it.

As I peacefully sat there, I saw two young girls walking in my direction. I knew them. They knew me. I'm the guy who is always working on his house. They're the girls who are always chasing after the young boys, play-fighting. Their play-fighting packs quite a wallop on those boys too. The boys however, just take their painful attention in stride, like young boys do.

When they reached the stairs, they saw me. "Hello girls," I said. They kept walking and didn't say a word. "Hello girls," I repeated. I thought that they were being a little dismissive, so I pushed it a bit. It's not like I was a <u>stranger</u>. I wanted to teach them a little neighborly etiquette. You know, "It takes a village" and all that.

One of the girls stopped and faced me, "Hey! We just saw you running near our friend's house" she affably offered. The other girl stopped behind her friend and unwillingly turned our direction, obviously annoyed that her walk was interrupted. "Yup I run a lot and I go to the gym too." I conversationally replied. "Working out is how you stay healthy and strong" I advised. (I thought I'd go for this teachable moment) Well the second girl stepped out from behind her friend and clearly had something to say. She planted herself in front position and then shifted her body weight to one leg. She put her hand on her hip, tilted her head to one side and pursed her lips as she looked me up and down and said, "You work out huh? Hmmmm, can't tell." She briskly turned away, took her friend's arm and marched off. The only thing she failed to do was to snap her fingers in a Z formation, "SNAP-SNAP-SNAP!"

There is no influencing or guiding some kids. There is definitely no chastising them. If you see one of your neighbor kids walking passed your house, and he or she decides to empty a bag of fries on your lawn, don't chide the child as so, "Oh no you didn't! Pick that up! What's wrong with you?" Never reprimand the kid. That's their mother's department. Scolding and scaring their child will be the end of you. Forget about the fathers defending their kid from this "strange man," their mothers will come over and read you to filth! So, if you've got a problem with the kid, speak to Mama. She'll make it right.

Also, do yourself a favor. Keep away from expressions like, "Wassup?" "Shit be dope!" "Oh hell naw," "Damn girl!" "Keep it real" and "Peace out homefry." It's not you. It never will be you. You're just a thin, pasty, middle-aged, gay guy. Wait a minute, that's me.

And boys, no matter how fit and ripped your abdominals are, no matter how hot the weather may be, never, ever wear your Hoochie Mama halter top and Daisy Dukes (jean shorts) when working in the yard, please! It will just scare the kids and freak out the adults. You are not a young, sexy Appalachian mountain girl. (If only wishing would make it so. I know dear)

WHERE ARE THE GAY BOYS?

It's been a few weeks since I started this writing project. Since that time, I have put my Art Deco Duplex on the market for sale. It is reasonably priced, given the many upgrades, with room for price and equity appreciation. I bought it for such a low price, with so much equity already in it, I can afford to leave some for the next guy. Most importantly, the rents can pay the mortgage, making this piece of income property a good deal. I admit, not as good a deal as when I bought it, but a good deal for a buyer who just wants to move in, or rent out, right away. Not everyone wants a project property.

With each passing day, and with each passing perspective buyer that viewed the property, I was reminded of why I wanted to write this book. Of the numerous interested buyers, there had been an Andrew, a Jeff, a Peter, a Das, a Durrell, and a Yuri. These boys were straight, which is fine of course, but I had hoped to see more interested gay boys.

All of these lads came for the same reason. They wanted to buy income property. I encouraged them, though I admit, somewhat self-servingly. Still, I praised them for their interest in income property. It's a smart way to go, and they knew it.

Some of these guys came with their girlfriends, wives, mothers and fathers. Ultimately, it was the women that decided not to write an offer. I asked two of the real estate agents involved what their clients thought of the property.

I was told, "His mother didn't like it," and "The wife didn't like it."
For many guys, women "rule the roost" or "run the show" (for you show girls). "Happy wife-happy life" is their code (Ok).

One Saturday morning, I got a call from guy named Patrick.
He told me that he and his "partner" were very interested, and that they thought the property looked <u>perfect</u> for them. I was pleased.
I thought I was finally hearing from a gay real estate investor.
The fact that he had an Irish name was an added amusement.

Five minutes into the conversation, Patrick told me that his partner was his <u>Dad</u>. Though I thought it was nice that they shared such a close relationship (certainly one I would want with my <u>own</u> father) I was, in all honesty, a little disappointed. Here I had yet another straight boy acting under the mentorship, attention and instruction of his father.

The next day, I had another father, "Stan." He was looking to buy a duplex for <u>his</u> son, who I later met. It was the son's girlfriend that doused that deal. He liked the property but she didn't- and that was that.

With this straight son/supporting father scene repeatedly played out before me, I kept thinking, "Where are the gay boys? They should be buying income property too. Where's their mentorship, attention and instruction?" This was the central theme of the book happening before my eyes. This was, and is, my observed, practical, empirical evidence for its writing. Where are the gay boys? They should be here too.

THE WINNERS

Where are you going to find a better investment than income property? It's a win-win-win.

First: your real estate investment is a physical "brick and mortar" property. It's not going to wilt into worthlessness like some high-priced, low-performing mutual fund.

Second: it's also paying you a financial return each month in the form of rental income. As soon as you start renting, you start making money. A (SFR) single family residence only pays you when you sell. Even then there is no making money unless the property has increased in value.

Third: the ultimate goal is realized when your property is sold and you make a significant profit- your win <u>fall</u>. That's going to feel great when your planning and hard work come together.

HELOC, NOT HE-MAN

As the expression goes, "Don't wait to buy real estate. Buy real estate and wait." As prices increase you will gain value in the property. With increased value, you gain equity. Equity is the difference between the home's fair market value and what you owe on the property (your mortgage). You could borrow against that equity and get a Home Equity Line of Credit that you could use to buy a second property (see pg. 107)

A Home Equity Line of Credit, or HELOC, is like a Revolving Line of Credit on your house. You can typically borrow up to 80% of the appraised value of your home minus the amount you owe.

For instance: Your property is appraised at $450,000. 80% of that is $360,000, but you owe $250,000 on it. The bank will give you a credit line of $110,000 or less (depending on your credit rating). Visit BankRate.com before you heloc shop.

You can pay it back over time (with monthly payments) or you can repay it in full at any time. Speaking of time, this isn't a 30-year deal, like some mortgages, though it's considered a second mortgage. There is a time limit, usually 5 to 10 years in which you can borrow the money. It's called, "the draw period."

A Revolving Line of Credit swings both ways. It decreases and increases as money is borrowed and repaid. It can be used over and over until you reach your limit, or until you repay it in full and close the account. The Revolver is a gay bar in Los Angeles. There, the door swings both ways. The men don't.

EQUITY AND LEVERAGING

Entering into the real estate market at an opportune time makes all the difference. Enter the market when it is depressed, not when it is thriving. As the economy improves, so does job growth, so does revenue, so does the real estate market, so does the value of your property. "A rising tide lifts all boats", John F. Kennedy. Consequently, you will gain value, equity and profit when you sell your investment. The property's equity increases as you make payments on your mortgage balance, and/or as the property value appreciates. This is what you want and need to happen if you are to realize your goal of financial solvency, strength and independence. That is NOT going to happen if you don't buy low. "Low-low-low-is-the-way-to-go! Where are those pom-poms when I need 'em?

Maybe you've already bought an inexpensive house. You have a very small monthly payment, and you've realized some equity appreciation. You already have a tenant paying your bills as well. That is the time you should be looking around for another property. With an easily manageable mortgage, some time as a homeowner/mortgage holder, and some equity in the property, you will able to borrow against the one to buy another. With your good credit and good mortgage payment history, you can apply for a Home Equity Line of Credit or a Cash Out Refi (nance). Speak to a Lender for all the options, the loan products.

When you borrow against the equity in your house to buy another house, it's called "Leveraging." Now, this is only, I repeat only, if you bought during a depressed market, or you got an excellent deal and your property has significantly increased in value, so that you're actually sitting on a heap of equity. In such a case, leveraging your property's equity to buy another is a manageable way to go (read on)

Unfortunately, "leveraging" is not a term I hear used that often these days. Most people aren't going out there leveraging their property. They're content with their ability to simply pay their current mortgage, never mind a second one.

I understand the desire to be careful, cautious, reserved, fearful even. I get it, but how far will that prudent posture take you? That's not how you become financially secure- if not rich- from real estate. Sometimes history can be the best teacher. To get some perspective, let's look back. Before the real estate market collapse of 2008-2012, many people made the mistake of borrowing against their houses, using their Home Equity Lines of Credit like an ATM, a Piggy Bank to buy whatever they desired. They thought their property would continue to increase in value and give them the money to pay for their latest cravings, but that's not what happened, quite the contrary. Many found their mortgage and their additional equity line of credit (which again is considered a second mortgage) to be more than their depreciated house was worth. Thus, the borrower became "upside down" in debt. Many defaulted on these loans. (p 71-73)

In an effort to avoid any future financial disaster, the Trump Tax Plan of 2018 rescinds the HELOC mortgage interest deduction, unless the borrower is specifically using it to improve their home, the collateral property- the property it is drawn from. I think that is reasonable, responsible, sensible, sound financial policy. It prevents people from recklessly spending, borrowing, burying themselves into debt, and potentially facing foreclosure. The problem is it costs the home owners and the investors/us, the gain from having that deduction. That's the downside, but don't be scared away by that change. I've used a heloc a number of times to help me purchase properties, and I would consider doing so again, even without the mortgage interest deduction. The objective is to buy a property that you're going to profit from. The loss of the M.I. deduction will have to be factored in, the cost of doing business. It's a small price to pay if it means getting a property with profit potential. Lastly, a heloc can definitely be used to improve the property once you/if you get it. Property improvement is an important part of our plan to help us make the profit. That's what we're working towards. If it is an investment property, or income property where you rent out units, almost everything is tax deductible, so keep those receipts. Those deductions will help offset the loss of your heloc mortgage interest deduction.

It's important to know about financial resources, about laws and policies that will affect your transactions and their profits. I encourage you to start paying attention to what's happening around you, specifically the jobs report, the housing market, mortgage interest rates, the stock market generally and the economic growth rate, which is a measure of a country's entire economic output, the total market value goods and services, the Gross Domestic Product, the GDP. As of the first quarter of 2019, the GDP was 3.2%. 2018 ended with 3.1% and 2017 with 2.3%. That's considered good compared to 2016 which ended at 1.5%, however, they're all anemic, impotent even, compared to China's growth rate of 6.4%. We have far more economic growth potential ahead of us. Remember, when the national economy grows, your personal economy grows as well. So, getta plantin' Farmer Femmy!

DOING THE MATH TO DETERMINE THE VALUE OF AN INCOME PROPERTY

Net Operating Income and Capitalization Rate

If you want to figure out your return, how much money you are making on your investment, consider the Capitalization Rate, or "CAP RATE", as they say in real estate/business lingo. It is the easiest and most used method. Rental property owners love to brag about their cap rate. "My cap rate is 5%." "Well mine is 10!" (size queens). Capitalization Rate is a good starting point when comparing investment opportunities. It's the interest you're going to make on your money- the return on your investment- the ROI. This is done by dividing the Net Operating Income, the NOI, by the Value (the price) of the property.

All the financial information of a property (particularly the cap rate and NOI) should be on the Selling Agent's Listing sheet, but, sometimes it's not. Even if it is, at some point you should take a few minutes to check their math. Those numbers, including the Asking Price, could be over or under. You need to know. You need to be sure they are correct, as those are the figures that will guide your decision on whether to buy or not. Assuming full occupancy, the common formula to arrive at the NOI is simply: 100 - 30 = 70.

Gross Scheduled Income (100% rents/fees/laundry) minus the Operating Expenses like taxes, insurance, utility expenses (take an average of 30% for those) leaves a remaining 70%, which is the Net Operating Income. 100 -30 = 70. The expense figure (the 30) is subject to change, given that some state's fees and taxes are more expensive than others. If you want to account for possible non-payment of rents or vacancies, take 3% (sometimes 5) off the top. 100 gets reduced to 97 and continue. (In rural areas, use 3 because there is less turnover)

The NOI is what you need to know, and now you know how they arrive at it. The important part is that you know and use the following formula to determine the CAP RATE. This is one you will use every time you consider an income property:

Cap Rate = Net Operating Income (NOI) / Value of the Property

Say you find a duplex that has an NOI of $36,000. It's priced at 250,000. Divide $36,000 by $250,000. What is your cap rate? It's 14.4%. Now that's something to brag about. What if you found another duplex across town? You like both properties equally, and they both need some work. The second property has an NOI of $19,000, and costs $175,000. Take 19,000 and divide by 175,000. It equals 10.8%.

Now you have the two Cap Rates to help you decide which property to pursue: 14.4% or 10.8 %? You can check the Market Value or Asking price of that property using the same figures.

Value = Net Operating Income (NOI) / Cap Rate

Take some time to understand use these formulas. Their results will help you decide how to proceed.

I recently reviewed one listing and found that the Agent miscalculated the Cap Rate. That error caused a $45,000 inflation of the Asking Price/Value. That difference is a provable number a Buyer could base their reduced offer on. Any feature of the property could be that difference, but in math, all features are equal. We don't care about the Greek garden statues in the back yard, or, maybe we do.

After you've scrutinized the cap rates of properties you're interested in, take a second look at two other factors: Rental Income and Property Value. Is there a growth or decline potential in the rental income? Based on our plan for improving a property, you should see only potential increase. You're in it to buy and improve the property, thereby increasing the rents, cap rate and value when you sell.

If there's not much room for improving the property, you probably shouldn't buy it, unless this is your second or third purchase and you're buying it for cash, then the amount of work you do is discretionary, not a necessary part of the plan to profit when you sell. You may not want to sell this one. You may want to keep it as income. It's all cash- your mad money. The same is true for the value of the property. You should only see a potential increase in value. You're not looking to buy the best house on the best block. What you're looking to buy is the worst house on the best block.

You're also not looking to buy the worst house on the worst block. That's not likely to increase in rental income, cap rate or property value. You may like a good project Butch, but hey- a slum is a slum. It's not likely to improve, unless there's a huge earthquake and it suddenly becomes beachfront property.

So again, consider CAP RATE as a tool to compare properties, and ultimately decide which one to purchase. You can think about the rental income and property value, but again, it's understood they will improve as the property improves. That's why you're there.

Gross Rent Multiplier

Now that you know what Cap Rate is (the return on your investment right?) you almost have to know this next one, the Gross Rent Multiplier, the GRM. The GRM helps you determine the market value (the price) of a property. Unlike Cap Rate, you want the GRM to be low- the lower the better. It is the <u>ratio</u> between the <u>price</u> of the property and its yearly gross <u>rent</u> (which is simply, the monthly rents x 12). It shows how many <u>years</u> a property will take to pay for itself by gross rents received. That's why lower is better, less time is needed. A higher GRM would indicate a poorer investment opportunity because <u>more</u> time is needed.

Most old school investors use the GRM as a simple rule-of-thumb to estimate a property's market value. The reason for its popularity is that it's so easy to calculate. The only drawback is that it's not always the most accurate as the Cap Rate, because it doesn't consider the cost of borrowing the money to buy the property, or even operating costs like utilities, taxes, insurance. That's why It's "gross" not "net." Still, despite its drawbacks, the GRM is a tool that can provide a quick and dirty, fast and loose, cheap and greasy way of comparing the market value to similar properties in the <u>same</u> area. There is no using GRM's for properties in different areas because those GRM's will be different, and won't provide you with usable, comparable information to determine the price of the property you want to buy. Here's how you use it.

GRM = Market Value (price) / Scheduled Gross Income (gross rents)

For example: the Market Value (price) of $750,000 divided by $36,000 of scheduled gross income = 20 GRM. It will take you 20 years of Gross Income to pay off this property.

Using the GRM

Let's say you're looking at a duplex to buy. You look at the recently sold, comparable properties in the area and found that their GRM's averaged around 25.

You can use <u>their</u> GRM to approximate the value of the property <u>you</u> want to buy. You learn that your property has an annual gross rental income of $32,000. Again, use the neighboring (comp) GRM with your Scheduled Gross Income.

GRM X SGI Income = Market Value

25 X $32,000 = 800,000

If it's listed for sale at $970,000, you'll know it's overpriced. If it's listed for $650,000, you know it's under-priced and could be in some sort of distress. This may be a property for you. Moreover, you learn the market value of the property based on its income, as compared to neighboring properties. Assuming there are no incredible, unusual or extraordinary features to your house, its value should be similar to neighboring properties. There's no guess work, no analysis paralysis. The numbers tell the tale.

The One Percent Rule is another quick way of evaluating a rental property. If the gross monthly rent (the rent before expenses) equals at least 1% of the purchase price, that is a good starting point, and merits further consideration and calculation. Say, you're looking to buy a condo for 200,000. If the gross monthly rent was $2,000, that would fall under the 1% rule. Just on first glance, that is a property an investor (you) would want to get more info on.

The Two Percent Rule. Well, it's not so much a "rule" as a guideline that some crafty real estate investors made up. The 2% rule says that for a rental property investment to be "good", the monthly rent should be equal to or higher than 2% of the purchase price. Ok. Ideally, this would be a suitable rule to use if you're looking to buy a property that has cash flow, but no real expectation for value increase, say in lower income areas with lower property values and lower rental values.

Cash flow is certainly beneficial, but we want to do better than that. We have a plan, and increasing a property's value is an important part of it. It's okay if your house is a little on the shabby side and is less desirable than the houses around it- actually it's preferable. You have an upside. For we investors, "Opportunity comes dressed in overalls," as Thomas Edison wrote, so put 'em on and get to work.

After you spruce it up, you will improve its desirability, marketability and profitability- which is our whole objective. Our plan, and the purchase price level we are after, considers the inherent risks: property age, condition, and location of the rental property. It's built in. We're not paying top dollar for a high-end property. We get that. We're there to make money. We're willing to take the risk, do the work and earn the rewards later.

CASH COW

When you have made enough money and you make an all cash purchase, your rental property will become a money-making machine, affectionately known as a, "Cash Cow". It won't be milk that is plentifully produced each month- it will be money. The rental money you make each month minus any bills is considered Net Spendable. It is also Passive Income, because it is not made from earned wages. It is your monthly Cash Flow, your Disposable Income, which is the amount of money you have to knock around with. It's all yours to do with as you will. Truth be known, our swanky, sophisticated fashion sense and smart hairstyles aren't the only reasons why some non-gays envy us. Quite simply, we have more money, more disposable income- for example, the acronym D.I.N.K.s. This was given to us by our straight (perhaps envious) married friends. D.I.N.K stands for Double Income No Kids. That's a name we can live with. We've been called worse, right?

It could be that you don't want to continue on this path of buying, improving, renting and/or and selling property. You don't want to be thought of as a, "Flipper!" That's so...unseemly. You were proactive early on and bought an inexpensive fixer that you remodelled and sold and made you a plentiful profit. You can't find another property that is cheap enough or distressed enough or "locationally" (a new adjective) tolerable enough, so you're considering another mortgage to help you buy a more expensive income property. With such a large down payment from the previous sale, your small mortgage will not be a burden to you. The monthly rent checks will easily carry the mortgage, and even earn you a net spendable.

Whether you put the proceeds of a sale into some other interest earning instrument, or you reinvest it in another income earning rental property, you have succeeded in becoming a smart, secure, self-sufficient, and self-supporting real estate investor. Great job!

www.shutterstock.com · 66374458

SOMEWHERE DIFFERENT

If you can't find a property in the areas you know, consider areas you <u>don't.</u> Some investors buy out of state and have management companies handle their property for a percentage of the gross monthly rents.

I was very interested in Ohio for a time. Columbus, for example, is a university town, so there is a steady tide of renters. It is also a very gay friendly and gay active city. You can buy a lot more for your money in the city of Columbus, than you can in the city of Los Angeles. If you don't choose to buy out of state with the profit you make from the sale of a house, you could stay where you are, knowing that it may take one or two times of buying on credit and selling for a profit, before you are able to make enough profit for an "all cash" purchase.

Keep at it. Remember what Sister Mary used to always say, "Repetidio Est Mater Studiorum" (Repetition is the mother of all studies, of learning). Repeatedly follow the plan and learn more as you go, until you have made enough money to purchase a property, or properties for cash.

FIRST TIME BUYER

The fact that you are a first-time buyer is a bonus. Also, it is much easier to qualify for a loan if you are going to be living <u>in</u> the property. It is called "Owner Occupied." It's almost a necessity, a condition for a loan, certainly for a first-time buyer.

As the Owner/Occupier of the property, you will be living in the property you are taking out a mortgage to buy and will always be on-site to care for it. No Lender is going to give you your first loan on a property that you don't plan on living in. It is more of a risk to them. Even if you are a seasoned borrower and this is your second house, lenders usually want you to be an Owner-Occupier.

A "seasoned borrower" is one who has consecutively paid one or more mortgages for at least two years. Don't be deterred if this is not you. All borrowers have their first loan, and this is yours. You are gainfully employed, have a source of income and have good credit, carry on.

If you are a younger gay buyer, having many working years ahead of you is an advantage when being considered for a mortgage, certainly for your first mortgage.

For us mid-career or retiring gays, we may have the advantage of having more money down, more assets to list, more credit experience (good for us). When you go back in a year or two, or three, looking for second mortgage to buy a second property, the lender will look at how seasoned you are, how consecutive and successful you were at paying your first mortgage.

BE OFFENSIVE

At one time, I had three mortgages, a home equity line of credit and three credit cards to pay each month. Admittedly, it was challenging at times, but well-worth the financial gain. That's what we're talking about here: how to achieve financial gain through real estate.

As with all credit, if you're going to be late, <u>tell</u> <u>them</u>. They're going to find out anyway. This is business, not a social event. It's nothing personal. They're not going to be <u>mad</u> at you. Having credit card companies calling you to find out <u>when</u> you're going to make your next payment, and to ask you <u>why</u> you're late is difficult and demoralizing. I know from personal experience. I also know from personal experience that it's better to call them <u>before</u> they call you. Give them something to document in your file. "I'm going to be late this month because... . I expect to be able to make my next payment...." "The best defense is a good offense" so goes that old football expression (yes football). You take it to them <u>before</u> they take it to you.

Also, it will strengthen you, empower you, knowing that you are correctly managing this debt. Yes, you owe the money, but you're not ignoring it or running from it. That shows integrity. Your self-respect is intact, well, for now anyways. Rest assured you're not the only person late with their payment. It may well turn out that the person on the other end of the phone has a helpful suggestion. That's quite possible. If they don't offer one- <u>ask</u>. The answer will always be "No", if you don't ask- so ask. These companies deal with calls like yours all day every day. Just 'fess up Buttercup. They may be able to help you.

Lastly, if when you call them, you get some jerk that just wants to beat you up over your financial difficulties- just hang up, call back, and speak to someone else. You're not speaking with the CFO of Bank of America. You're speaking with a clerk sitting in a row of cubicles, with a phone and a computer. Their power comes from their knowledge of your debt, and your desire to pay it and maintain your credit score.

I've had reasonable collection clerks. I've had rude ones. They've got their job to do, we know that, but verbal abuse is not a call requirement- just hang up, call back, and speak to someone else. I've done it, and it made all the difference.

If you have to, you can always call upon your inner "Sassy Black Woman." She'll knock that callous collector down a peg or two.

A LENDER FOR YOU

For some of you the idea of qualifying for a mortgage, and then actually being responsible for it, seems a little intimidating, scary. You can relax. It's not. It is however, a process, one that you will be lead through. It's just a matter of getting some information together and letting your Lender (banker, or mortgage broker) do their job.

You will be greeted, invited, hosted, welcomed with open arms by all: private lenders, banks, credit unions, mortgage brokers all vying for your business. They want your gay dollar. They've got to make a living too.   If they don't write loans, they don't make their money, and they have their own bills to pay.

Be assured, they'll be very pleased to see your eager, prepared, gay, friendly self, walking through their door to discuss real estate financing with them.

LESS IS MORE

I had a client who needed a loan. I referred him to a Mortgage Broker that I've worked with. She is a smart, patient, lovely woman. I thought she'd take good care of him. Instead of going and meeting with her personally, he decided to email her, which was fine. He emailed her alright...ad nauseam. He emailed her his entire life story, including tales of his alcohol abusing father who, "never loved" him, his faithful, co-dependent mother who, "should have left him years ago", his older brother who is in prison for dealing drugs, and his "baby sister" who had two babies of her own and now lives with their parents. Also, there was one seemingly <u>endless</u> account about his younger, crystal meth using, on and off again ex-boyfriend who stole credit cards, cash and jewelry from him over the span of the last five years.

Really? This is how you want to present yourself to someone, someone you don't know, someone you want to borrow money from? It was a complete turn off. That smart, patient, lovely Mortgage Broker said to me in a befuddled manner, "I can't do anything with him."

So friends, please remember, "Less is more." The <u>less</u> you say the better. Don't get all... dramatic! You're not there to spill your guts or share family secrets. This is <u>not</u> an opportunity to purge your anxiety and neurosis. The Mortgage Broker is not your Therapist. They will learn what they need to know from your application, your credit report and a few questions at your meeting. For that matter, when you go in to meet with your Lender, look nice. Wear a shirt and jacket, maybe a tie, and take it easy on the cologne. "Clothes make the man," so make it a good impression.

It won't change any negatives you may have on your credit report, but it <u>will</u> make a difference in how you are received and regarded. It will also leave open a door for suggestions and possibilities as well.

A side note: If you've got someone stealing from you, don't wait five years to get rid of him. Show him the door now. You've got places to go. You're moving up. You don't need someone keeping you down.

GOOD AND BAD CREDIT

Good credit is money you borrow to pay for the necessities of life: a safe comfortable place to live, a car to commute to work, a higher education. Good credit is almost always cheaper and loaned at a much lower interest rate. It is usually tax deductible, certainly for your home. You can deduct the interest you pay on your mortgage and/or a second mortgage. (see pages 106-107)

If it is an income property, you can deduct almost every dollar you spend on it. In order to take these deductions, these "write offs," you need to claim the rent as (taxable) income, and then you can deduct your property related expenses to, "offset" that income tax. Get it?

Bad credit is money you borrow on your credit card to buy something you want but really can't afford. For example: all that camping equipment in your attic, the Bow Flex that's still boxed in your garage, or that His and His pair of red leather Lazy Boy Recliners in the den.

You didn't really <u>need</u> any of those things. You could have waited. Instead, you thoughtlessly put them on your charge card and are currently defaulting on their debt. Consequently, you are unable to get approved for any new credit. Lenders want nothing to do with you. Your credit default file gets turned over to a collection agency. Bad credit could result in bankruptcy filings and vehicle repossessions. There's nothing <u>good</u> about that.

When Good Credit is Bad

In a sense, even good credit is bad. Once you borrow money to finance good, important, necessary things, you are obligated to a repayment plan. That money is being taken off the table, out of circulation. It is spent already. It is current and future income needed to pay off the first debt. That money could very well have been used for something else, something more fun and exciting. Consequently, you miss opportunities. You can't afford to pay for that luxurious, exotic, tropical, secluded stay in Fiji, if you're already on the hook to pay for that new hybrid, career-commuting car. Those warm, intoxicating, orchid scented breezes are going to have to wait...bummer.

When Bad Credit is Good

Bad credit is good because when that debt is paid back, it contributes to your healthy credit score and increased credit availability. You're able to borrow even more of it, if you pay it back as promised. That's good.

RENTAL INCOME AND LOAN QUALIFICATION

Loan Qualification

Each month, you collect rents. It is rental income. Can the rental income be considered as mortgage-qualifying income when you apply for a loan? The short answer is "Yes." Well, first it was "Yes", then it was "No." Now it's "Yes" again. How's that for brevity?

Now the longer answer: Before the real estate meltdown of 2008, and the subsequent economic fall out, you could buy a rental property and immediately use its rental income to help qualify for a loan. This was a direct benefit to purchasing income property. (It's how I bought my first three income properties). The lender would assume that some part of the rental income, usually 70%, would remain after paying for taxes, insurance and maintenance costs. Following the financial crises, the rules changed. Lenders could not allow rental income to be used as mortgage-qualifying income, until <u>after</u> it was on your tax return for at least a year. That didn't do you much good if you <u>needed</u> the income to help you buy the place that will <u>generate</u> the income.

Now we're back to the "Yes." It's the same as it was before. Generally, lenders will allow you to use the 70% of your rental income to qualify for non-owner-occupied property.

For example, say you want to buy a Triplex. Each unit rents for, say, $1200. Take 3 x $1200 = $3600 monthly x 0.70 = $2520 net. You could use $2520 a month of rental income to qualify for your mortgage. (that's a good $30,240 a year).

SFR's

What if you don't buy a duplex or multi-unit property? If you can only purchase a <u>single-family residence,</u> an "SFR", you need to designate that property as your primary residence. You buy it, live in it, maybe rent out a room to have some additional money coming in, improve it, then rent and/or sell it.

Tax Savings

There is another reason of principal importance to live on the property, and consequently benefit from a substantial tax savings. It is detailed in the <u>BILL'S RULE</u> chapter on page 150. (Look for Bill Clinton's friendly wave).

Down Payment

Living on the property also affects the down payment amount. Investment Property loan down payments are usually much higher. Since the economic crisis, the down payment requirements have been raised. Today 5% down is acceptable for a borrower with good credit who is purchasing a "primary residence." The same borrower purchasing it as an "investment property" used to have to put 20% down. You may have to <u>make</u> it your primary residence, if coming up with the additional 15% is not possible.

<u>Here's a new, helpful option</u>: As of Nov, 2023, Fannie Mae (which a gov't program that backs mortgage loans) has lowered its required down payment on owner occupied multi-family properties from 15% and 25% to just <u>5%</u>. So, now just 5% is needed to get you in! That's a good deal!

In Hard Times

There's a reason why our plan focuses on, and is most successful on, investment property. You have more options when you have <u>other people's</u> <u>money,</u> when you are not carrying the full financial weight. This is particularly important when you're just starting out with your first property and you haven't yet realized any financial gain. You <u>need</u> an additional cash flow to help pay the bills and improve the property. Having an additional income source will help you- and if necessary- <u>carry</u> you.

I don't want to spend too much time on this. Actually, I didn't really want to mention it because it sounds negative, but it <u>is</u> important. O.P.M. will C.Y.A. This is just a thought to hold on to, to keep in your back pocket, next to your fuchsia and dark pink hankies. (Google it)

If you suddenly, fearfully find yourself out of job, the rental income can keep your boat afloat, can be your financial lifesaver. It's a frightening and distressing predicament to lose a job, especially when you have serious bills to pay.

Here's the good news: If you followed the plan and purchased a property for a low price, then improved it (gained equity) and rented it out, you have steady rental income each month. Put any additional improvement projects on hold for now. Use that rental income to pay your bills.

Though it's not what you thought or wanted your real estate investment to be, it <u>is</u> a relieving, freeing, immediate source of money. It is an investment property that you don't have to <u>sell</u> to earn money from, like you would from a single-family residence.

Your investment property can be your supporting source of income in your hour of need. Again, it wasn't what you wanted this investment to be, however it is an acceptable and appreciated alternative to defaulting on your bills and your mortgage. Now, go out there and find another job.

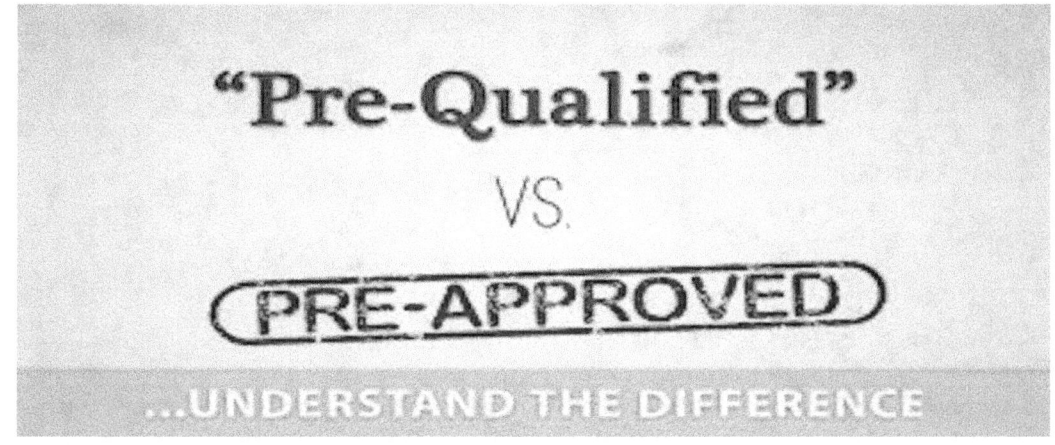

PRE-QUALIFY vs. PRE-APPROVAL

It is at the initial meeting with your Lender, Loan Representative or Mortgage Broker that you are Pre-qualified. You simply tell your Lender your overall financial picture, including your debt, income and assets. It does not include an analysis of your credit report. Based on that information, they will give you an idea of the mortgage amount you qualify for.

Pre-qualification can be done over the phone or Internet, and it usually doesn't cost a thing. It does <u>not</u> carry the weight of importance that a Pre-Approval does.

Getting Pre-Approved is the next step. It's the real deal. It is much more involved, more comprehensive. You will complete an official mortgage application, usually with an application fee. You will supply them with records of your income and of your debt. At the end of this process, you will receive a conditional commitment in writing for an exact loan amount. You'll also have a better idea of the interest rate you will be charged on the loan. That's the goal here.

With pre-approval, you won't be looking at properties you may well-like but cannot well-afford. No one's time is wasted. You will know, the Real Estate Agents will know, and of course your Lender will know the loan terms

With a Pre-Approval Letter accompanying the Purchase Agreement, your offer on a property will be taken seriously and immediately. As American essayist and poet, Ralph Waldo Emerson wrote, "<u>The future belongs to those who prepare for it</u>." Believe me, if you see a property that you really want, <u>you</u> will want to be seen as the Buyer who is prepared. So, get 'er done.

PROVE IT!

Income over two years

Report how much you earn and how you earn it. For example, is your income from salary, bonuses, commissions, interest income or dividends? You will need to bring your most recent pay stub, previous year's W-2 forms and tax returns.

Employment history

Job stability is a factor that a mortgage lender will look for. This is not an absolute requirement, but at least two years on a job would be best. If you change jobs but stay in the same line of work, you shouldn't have a problem. For example, I was a Teacher in one school, then left after five years for another school. My career stayed the same, which showed stability.

Credit score

A Credit Score is a numerical value that grades your credit risk at a given point in time. It is based on a statistical evaluation of information in your credit history that has been proven to be predictive of how well you handle the loan.

It is part of your Credit Report, which is a detailed account of your credit history. It allows lender or other businesses to examine your use of credit. It provides information on money that you've borrowed from creditors (who you owe money to) and your payment history (how well you've paid them back).

Paradoxically, ironically, "oxymoronically" (another new adjective) the more you available credit you have, the more they'll offer you. You would think the credit card companies would want to limit your credit card availability to keep you from overspending, but not so. Provided you pay it back as scheduled, they will fill your mailbox with credit card offers. You will need to spend judiciously, cautiously, carefully. Leave your credit cards at home when you're stepping out to The Anvil, Cuffs, Driveshaft, Eagles, Rage, Probe, Trash, Spit, Spike or wherever you carouse. You're out to establish some good credit here, not establish yourself as a Sugar Daddy. That'll come later.

If you don't have any credit cards, you can start with a store charge card. My first card was with Sears. You can also start with a Secured Credit Card. I started with a secured Visa.

A secured card requires a cash collateral deposit that becomes the credit line for that account. For example, if you put $300 in the account, you can only charge up to $300. You will make payments with interest on the money you borrowed, were credited, even though it's <u>your</u> money.

You will demonstrate your ability and responsibility in managing this debt. It will establish a credit history on you. Make it a good start. Do this correctly (pay on time) and you will soon be getting offers from <u>un</u>secured credit cards in the mail.

Check Bankrate.com for a list of secured credit card issuers. This site is an excellent source of all things credit- Bookmark it. If you're a credit union member, ask about a secured card there. About half of the nation's credit unions offer secured cards to their members and may offer lower interest rates and waive annual fees.

Not all banks offer these types of credit cards. Banks make more money if they offer <u>un</u>secured credit cards with lower limits and higher interest rates and fees.

Debt Information

Despite what you hear, it's okay to have debt. It's how much debt you have - the ratio of debt to available credit - that matters most. Usually 30% of your credit limit is considered good. Your lender will need to know the balances and account numbers of your current loans and debts, including student loans, car loans, credit card balances and any other loans you may have.

If you don't have any debt- get some. I have a neighbor who prides himself on only paying cash for everything. While that may sound like a noble feat, it is not. It is a naïve one. Debt and repayment are necessary to your goal of purchasing real estate, and ultimately selling it for a profit. You need to establish a credit history, of borrowing on credit and repaying with interest. This will demonstrate that you are responsible with money and will positively affect your credit score and credit worthiness.

Credit Reports are used by banks, credit unions, credit cards, stores and other lenders to estimate the risk a company takes on by giving you a loan. It scores the likelihood of you making payments on time in the next two to three years. Usually the higher the score, the less risk the person represents. Credit Reports tell a story. This is where that wild, never-to-be-forgotten, White Party weekend in Palm Springs, rears it's never-was-fully-paid-for ugly head.

If you don't know your credit score, you can go to AnnualCreditReport. com and get one free yearly report from each credit bureau. A Credit Report provides all the information in your credit file that is kept by a consumer reporting company. Information is reported to lenders when you apply for credit, and they "run your credit."

The three Credit Bureaus are called: Equifax, Experian and TransUnion. Your credit score also show how likely you are to consistently pay the mortgage debt. Credit scores: typically, 680-724 is considered good, 725-759 is very good, and 760-850 is considered excellent. If your score is not where you want it to be, there are things you can do.

Steps you can take to improve your credit rating

- Always pay your bills on time.

- Don't use more than 10-30 % of your available credit. The farther you are from your credit limit, the better.

- Don't apply for cards just to see if you'd get it.

- Don't cancel cards you're not using.

- The longer a card stays open, the better your score.

- By leaving unused credit cards open, you are showing credit availability, untapped resource.

Disputable Charges

When you get a copy of your credit report, give it a careful read.
Do you recognize all the charges on it? You're a little baffled because
you can't find those $6000 Majesty Prestigio golf clubs, or the $8,400
Louis Vuitton golf bag. What about those $5,000 John Lobb golf
shoes, the $375 Oakly sunglasses, or the three $165 Lindeberg golf
shirts? Hmmmm.

You're a little concerned about your long-term memory, but then you
remember... you don't <u>play</u> golf. Then you remember something else,
rather some<u>one</u> you forgot; that the tall, tan, chiselled, thirty-something
year old Adonis who you met by the hotel pool, who wouldn't stop
waxing on about his golf game, who was in town for the Palm Springs
Stonewall Golfers Tournament, and who later joined you for a
"nightcap" in your bungalow <u>did</u>. And you wondered why you didn't
see him by the pool for the rest of the weekend (you suave Silver
Daddy).

Now you have a little work to do. You need to contact the agency that provided you the credit report and dispute those charges. Remember, less is more. Don't share all the lascivious, lurid details, "Just the facts, ma'am," as Joe Friday on <u>Dragnet</u> used to say. (No, that's a different kind of drag Rupaul).

"Some guy stole my credit card and ran up all these charges, etc... ." Don't get nervous. You're not guilty of anything. You're the <u>victim</u> here. You're not going to get the third degree. Your answers will <u>not</u> sound like this, "Was he what? Was he handsome? Sure, he was beauti... I don't think it's any of your business what he was doing in my room. Yes, he was younger than I but that's not relevan... No, I think he left before dawn. No, I didn't have my wallet on my person. <u>He</u> was on my person!" Well! Fear not. Your claim will be processed and those charges will be deleted from your credit report. That could have been an expensive lesson to learn. Ahh, the power of a pretty face. "It is amazing how complete is the delusion that beauty is goodness," Leo Tolstoy (who by the way was not at <u>all</u> pretty, sounds like he was bitter about it)

The FTC

For ID Theft, Privacy and Security issues, visit the Federal Trade Commission website. This website explains a comprehensive list of issues and advises you how to handle them: Identity Theft, Your Rights in Credit Reporting, Credit Cards and Consumer Loans, Credit Scoring, Credit Repairing, Mortgages and Real Estate, Lending Practices and Scams just to mention a few. I suggest you visit their webpage, and bookmark it for future use. It is: FTC.GOV.

As the webpage says, "So read up! Education is the first line of defense against fraud and deception. It can help you make well-informed decisions before you spend your money." "And that's the truth," Edith Ann.

Personal Assets

(No, this is not your "money maker") Personal assets are balances and recent statements of any bank accounts, including checking and savings. Stocks, bonds, certificates of deposit, retirement funds, life insurance cash values and personal property values, like cars and boats, are also personal assets and are all factored in when calculating your credit worthiness.

If you don't have any of these assets yet, don't worry, you will. In my experience, real estate has been the secure, profitable, physical asset that has made all subsequent, succeeding, successive assets possible. First comes property. The rest will follow. You will see.

MORTGAGES

A mortgage is a loan secured by real property, by real estate.
A mortgage note evidences the existence of the loan. In everyday usage, the word "mortgage" alone is most often used to mean mortgage <u>loan</u>.

As I'm sure you'll remember from your Latin studies, the word stem, "mort" means death- as in mortal, mortality, mortally, mortician, mortuary, mortuous, or Morticia (Addams of course).

The word mortgage is a French Law term meaning "death pledge" meaning that the pledge dies (or ends) when the obligation is fulfilled or it dies by foreclosure due to lack of payment: death, done, ended, over, as in, "If you don't pay back this loan you're dead to me and I'm taking your house," over.

A Conventional Loan takes forever to die, usually 30 years. It is generally the preferred loan. These types of loans look much more promising to a Seller if they are considering multiple offers. Sometime deals get made <u>not</u> just over <u>price</u>, but over which deal is likely to get funded and close. Once conventional loans get approved, they normally close. That's what you want. You <u>won't</u> want <u>your</u> deal to die.

RATES AND TERMS AND POINTS (OH MY!)

Rate is the percentage rate the bank charges you on the money they loan you (simple enough). Along with a rate quote, comes an APR, or Annual Percentage Rate. This figure represents the actual yearly cost of the money borrowed over the term of a loan. This includes any fees or additional costs associated with the transaction. It provides you with a "bottom line number," so you can easily compare rates charged by other potential lenders.

Term is the length of time they give you to pay the loan back. Mortgages are typically for 30 years at a fixed rate. Again, that is termed the "Conventional" loan.

There is usually the option of a 15-year loan, if you have good money coming in, but 30 years is the norm. Over a 30 years term, your monthly payments will be smaller but the amount of money you are actually paying back is significantly more, because you're paying interest over a longer period of time.

When you become a more seasoned borrower, you may be able to refinance (which is to get a new loan for a different rate, and possibly, term).

Points. There are two different kinds of points: Discount Points and Origination Points.

Discount points are like upfront money, prepaid interest really. You get a discount on the interest rate, because you are paying for it up front. The more points you pay, the cheaper your loan will be. It is a fee based on 1% of the loan's value.

Say you borrow, $100,000. A point would be 1% of that, or $1000.00. On a $200,000 loan, a point will be $2000, on a $300,000 loan, $3000 etc. See Bankrate.com for loan rates. Remember, bookmark that site on your computer. You're going to want to refer to it occasionally.

Origination Points are a processing fee. This is what you pay to the lender or loan officer for their role in evaluating, processing and approving your mortgage loan. Unlike the other types of points (for example, discount points), origination points are not tax deductible. Like discount points, a single origination point represents 1% of the mortgage loan. For example, if you are borrowing $150,000 and the bank is charging you 1.5 origination points, you will end up paying $2,250 (or 1.5% of $150,000).

The amount of the origination points are not set in stone. You may be able to negotiate them down a little, particularly if you have a good credit rating- but you've got to ask. When I purchased my second property, I had the gall, the gumption, the courage, the chutzpah, the <u>nerve</u> to ask for a reduction in origination points- and I got one! Again, if you don't ask the answer will always be, "No" - so ask

Though he may to play "hard-to-get," he is not. The Lender will understand that you are well-positioned to borrow money, and that you could just as easily go somewhere else. They may cut you a break to keep you seated at his desk. Remember, he's got to make a living too.

DOWN PAYMENTS AND PROGRAMS

A down payment is a percentage of your home's value. Depending on the type of mortgage/loan program you apply for, your down payment can range from 0 to 20%, or more if you have the money.

FHA/FEDERAL HOUSING ADMINISTRATION

The Federal Housing Administration or "FHA" is a government owned insurance company that insures home loans from FHA approved lenders for buyers who cannot afford a conventional down payment. FHA backed loans allow a home buyer to purchase a property with as little as 1/2% up to 3% down.

The lower down payment requirement generally attracts many lower income and/or first-time homebuyers. If you're a little light on your down payment, tell your Realtor that you're looking for an FHA property.

FHA loans are only available on specific properties and only in some areas. FHA properties can be in less desirable areas, or can be in some sort of distress, like a foreclosure or short sale.

The FHA 203K -loan program allows borrowers to add funds to their FHA loans for rehabilitation, home improvements or repair work. So, if you find yourself a distressed FHA property, there is an additional source of money for those renovations.

There is a catch to this supportive pitch. To get a mortgage from the Federal Housing Administration, there is a one-time, upfront mortgage insurance premium, a fee. It is equal to 1.75 % of the loan amount. There is also a monthly mortgage insurance premium fee that is based on the terms of your loan.

This isn't free money. This is a way to pick up and fix up a property that you ultimately sell and profit from. You can then move on to the next property, and so on, until you won't even need a loan to buy a property. Again, that's the objective of our plan.

VA LOANS

The Veterans Administration provides our Veterans, or those on active duty in the military, a loan program with no down payment, no private mortgage insurance and no closing costs. This is a very helpful, supportive and well-deserved way to go if you serve (ed) your country in the military.

OWNERS WILL CARRY

Sometimes you will see an advertisement for a property that's for sale that says, "Owner Will Carry". Huh? Carry what? Carry who? This means that the Owner/Seller will, "Carry the Note", or "Hold the Paper," and act as the bank to finance the Buyer's (your) purchase of his property.

That sounds good to you! With your terrible credit, you've all but given up on buying your own home. Now suddenly this new way of financing is available to you. You're very excited! With this method, you won't have to pay the application fee, the origination fee, the appraisal fee, the document preparation fee, the tax fee, or the flood fee. Free-free-free-free-free-free! Fantastic! This is it! This is the golden key to finally unlock the doors of Homownership! Boy, you have finally <u>arrived</u>! You are here and queer and you have no fear! Yeeee Haaaaw!

Hold your horses Cowboy! Before those Wrangler Jeans get too tight. Keep that pistol holstered. Now take a deep breathe...okay. This is <u>not</u> the way to buy a property. You need to know this immediately, make that <u>immediately</u>! It sounds like a trouble-free way to go, but when you understand the facts, you'll soon learn it has a disastrous downside. Sure, it may get you in. It may be <u>easy</u>, but it won't be <u>cheap</u>. I know you're used to those two working together, but here they don't. This is a "last ditch effort," and everyone knows it. This is a very risky, expensive and desperate way to buy real estate, and "Desperation" is a foul cologne to wear there partner.

You want to become, "Mr. Buyer." You see your family, friends, and co-workers buying property. That gives you a case of F.O.M.O - Fear Of Missing Out. You feel like you're missing out. There is one major obstacle: your poor spending habits, lack of attention, and maybe some bad luck (it happens) have earned you a poor credit rating.

You've tried everything. You've even tried <u>chanting</u> over it. "I <u>see</u> the house. I <u>will</u> the house. I am <u>one</u> with the house." No Grasshopper - you're not.

While your spirit is admirable, your strategy is not. Buying a property isn't something you just <u>do</u>. You work up to it. You prepare. You certainly don't do it when you're in an inferior financial position. Mr. Seller can make lots of money carrying the note/holding the paper, because he is lending to someone who can't get a loan anywhere else but is still hungry and anxious to buy.

Here's how it works:

The Seller will often charge full retail price for the home. There is no negotiating the price down.

He will carry the note and charge you a higher interest rate, near double the interest rate a traditional lender would charge.

He will require/demand a substantial down payment of 20-30%, or more if he thinks he can get it from you. It's more negotiable with a traditional lender.

If you don't have the down payment, you will pay a much higher price and higher monthly mortgage payment. With no money of your own invested, no, "skin in the game," the Seller will be assuming all the risk. That's going to cost you.

Though the money will be calculated for a shorter time period (the term) it must be paid in full in 3-5 years (depending on the Lender/Seller)

The thinking on that is, that while the buyer is repaying the loan/making good on his debt, he will also be improving his credit score while gaining equity in the property. These financial improvements might enable him to get a traditional mortgage, so as to pay off the seller's more <u>expensive</u> loan that he took on just to buy the place.

Now, here's the rub (not that kind of rub). If Mr. Buyer can't make the expensive mortgage payments, Mr. Seller forecloses on Mr. Buyer and calls Mr. Sheriff to evict him from the house. Mr. Buyer can keep all his belongings, but he loses that hefty down payment of 20-30%. The dirty little secret is...are you ready? Mr. Seller is glad this happened to Mr. Buyer. He keeps all that deposit money and he keeps his house. He will then find another unprepared, uneducated, unarmed chump who is desperate to buy.

You won't be that chump. This won't happen to you. You are preparing yourself and won't fall for such a foolish, possibly ruinous offer. As the Latin proverb states, "Praemonitus, praemunitus." "Forewarned is forearmed." You'll know better. After a few years, when you have earned the title, "Rich Bitch," you may want to be on the top end of this deal, and be the bank, the lender, "the pitcher" as it were. I expect by then you'll have at least one or two properties that are paid for. You could put one of them up for sale, hold the paper, and find your own unprepared, uneducated, unarmed desperado to buy it.

Your Buyer hasn't really thought it through and doesn't have a Mentor to advise him. He buys the house. He defaults. You make some obscene profit off this ignorant innocent. You keep your property and his money. You enjoy a penthouse view and spend your days hosting martini luncheons on your yacht, while he lives at the Downtown Mission and pan handles on the Melrose exit of the 101. I hope you're happy with yourself Cruella!

WHEN TO WAKE UP

If mortgage interest rates start going up, you should <u>wake</u> up. They shouldn't rise until the real estate market starts looking very favorable, sustainable, healthier. That may signal a time for you to jump into the market, if you haven't already.

If you didn't get in at the bottom, at least you'll be <u>closer</u> to the bottom, with still some potential for an increase in property value, thus an increase in equity. If not lowest, get in while it's still low<u>er</u>.

I liken this to people who wait for, "the perfect property". Perfection may never come, neither may your perfect interest rate. Of course, you will run the numbers and make sure you can afford your monthly payment, but don't wait for the rates to hit rock bottom. You may be waiting a very long time. The important part is that you buy a property, that you "have a position", as they say on Wall Street.

If property values go up, you will gain equity and will be able to refinance later. I did that a couple of times. My first rate of 7.75%, which is not low, but it was lower compared to the double-digit rates of the late 1980's. Also, when rate are higher, there is less competition to buy. That should keep the purchase prices down.

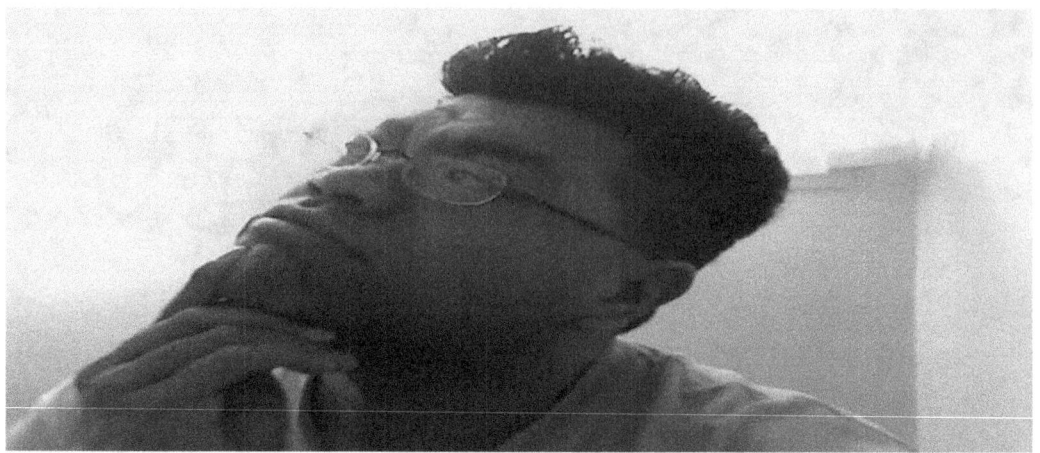

EYES OPEN

As I am encouraging you, I'm also looking around for an inexpensive property investment for myself. It so happens that my own neighbors are losing their house. Maybe this was by choice. Sometimes people can't stomach the loss in value on a property they once had high hopes for, so they're willing to walk away and let the bank have it. Sometimes also, homeowners let their "hobbies" get in the way of their actual bills (those darn bills).

While I am sorry my neighbors are losing their house, they'll recover somewhere else. In truth, the house is in deplorable condition. There's nothing good about it. It's blight on the neighborhood, a "shonda for the neighbors," for you Yiddish language lovers. (I know you're out there. I'm one of you). My neighbors didn't keep their house up, so consequently, it has kept <u>down</u> the neighborhood's desirability.

This would be a good house to invest in. "Buy the worst house on the best street," is certainly true here. If you see a house in disrepair but the neighboring houses are all well maintained, just on face value, you're looking at a good investment. Its terrible condition means there is that much more time, work and money that will have to be spent on reconditioning it. Its terrible condition also means you will get it for a cheaper price.

Again, if you see the rest of the neighborhood in good shape, your good timing and hard work will definitely capitalize (make the most from) your investment.

TAX PERKS TO (RENTAL) PROPERTY OWNERSHIP

Ugh, the very thought of taxes zones me out. Where am I? Well, thank goodness there are professionals in this field who can lead the charge here. I am definitely not one of them. When your tax time comes around, definitely speak to a tax professional for advice and tax law updates. I've had the same smart, savvy, sister girl doing my taxes for years. She knows my story and helps me tell it to the IRS. You probably have a tax pro of your own. If you don't, get someone you feel comfortable with and stay with them. Give them your business. Be loyal to them and they will be loyal to you.

I do know a few things about taxes that I can share with you, though I'm going to need a pot of coffee to keep me on message. Here goes... When you buy a property, be it a condo, duplex, residence, townhouse or tee pee, there are some standard tax deductions. Just a reminder, a tax deduction is a reduction of your total income, which decreases the amount of money used in calculating the tax due.

For example, if an individual takes advantage of a $1,000 tax deduction on $50,000 worth of taxable income, his or her taxable income is reduced to $49,000.

Mortgage Interest Deduction: Maybe the biggest tax break you will have will come from owning a home, from carrying a mortgage. With the Mortgage Interest, or "M.I." deduction, you are able to deduct from your taxes the amount of interest you pay on your yearly home mortgage. It's usually a sizeable amount. It is the M.I. tax deduction that promotes home ownership. Without it, many people would stop buying homes. Home building and buying creates jobs. With no jobs, no money changes hands. Economic growth is stifled and contributes to recession.

Presently, you are allowed to deduct the M.I. for houses up to $750,000. Anything over that, you start paying the M.I. (This is a problem to wealthy buyers who want higher mortgage interest from more expensive real estate to offset their income tax- but that's a quality problem. We're not there just yet)

Points: When you buy a house, you usually have to pay "points" (fees) to the lender to get your mortgage. (Refer back to Points page 135). They are also tax deductible.

Taxes: You can deduct the local property taxes you pay each year.

P.M.I: Buyers who make a down payment of less than 20% of a home's cost Usually get stuck paying a premium called, Private Mortgage Insurance, or "P.M.I." PMI is an extra fee that protects the lender if the borrower fails to repay the loan. I've had to pay P.M.I. before. It's an added expense. No one likes it. No one wants it, but it's the cost of doing business. Currently, it's tax deductible too, so that makes it an easier pill to take, to chew, to swallow.

When you do go shopping for a lender, armed with a good credit score, and a well - priced property with some built in equity, you may be able to find one who will <u>not</u> charge you P.M.I. Keep that in mind.

Loans are financial products that are put on the open market and must be sold. To get the business, some lenders have a "No P.M.I" products. I know they're out there. Look for them when you're looking for a mortgage.

Penalty-free Traditional IRA Payouts:

(Attention you Mid-career and Retiring gays). As a further incentive to homebuyers, Congress offers to waive the normal 10% penalty for first-time homebuyers who withdraw cash from traditional IRAs before age 59 1/2. At any age, you can with - draw up to $10,000 penalty-free, to buy or build a first home for yourself.

Roth IRA can be of help here too. The government allows you to withdraw from your Roth IRA, tax and penalty free, at any time and for any reason.

Once the account has been opened for at least five years, you can also withdraw up to $10,000 of earnings, tax and penalty free, to buy a first home.

If you are purchasing rental property, there are other deductions you can take. If you live on the property, then you may only be entitled to a fraction of the deductions, because a part of this rental property is also your primary residence.

Depreciation is an annual allowance for the wear and tear, deterioration, obsolescence, and uselessness of the property. Depreciation reduces your basis for calculating the gain or loss on a later sale. It takes place over time according to an I.R.S. schedule: 27 1/2 years for a residential rental property and 39 years for a commercial property.

Improvements and Repairs

Property improvements are also included in the cost basis (the cost of the house) and are depreciated over time. Improvements add to the value of a property. They prolong the useful life or adapt it to new uses.

Property repairs are deductible in the year they occur. The repairs maintain your property in good condition. They don't necessarily improve it.

Operating Expenses

Routine expenses that keep a property going are also deductions. You can also deduct interest on loans for improvements (like a Home Equity line of Credit) and the interest on credit cards used as part of your rental activity, like your Home Depot card.

Home Depot: where the men are helpful, handsome, and hunky. Lowes... not so much.

There are also allowable deductions for local property taxes, insurance, property management fees, advertising and utilities, assuming that the tenants don't pay them. Unfortunately, Home Owner's Association fees are not tax deductible.
(They should be)

All deductible expenses must be what the IRS deems as ordinary and necessary. Don't go crazy. Keep it real, or real-<u>ish</u>.

Travel

You can deduct travel expenses associated with rental property, whether they involve driving cross-town or flying cross-country.

For local travel, you can deduct the actual expenses: gasoline, upkeep, repairs, or use the standard mileage rate.

If you're gassing up to go to your rental property a few hours away, or you're refilling a rental truck needed for that rental property, both the gas and the truck are deductible from your taxes. Tolls and parking are also deductible. It's a good idea to keep the receipts. By the end of the tax year, they will accumulate to an amount well-worth their keeping.

For overnight travel, you can deduct airfare and hotel bills, and part of your meals and other expenses. You might even be able to mix business with pleasure if you properly prorate and document the business expenses. Again, don't go crazy.

Deducting your admission to <u>Blow Buddies</u> while visiting a San Francisco triplex is not going to pass muster, will definitely <u>not</u> pass the tax test. Don't try it.

Home Office

If rental business is conducted out of your home, you may be able to deduct certain expenses, including a portion of utilities, long distance phone calls and office supplies.

To qualify, the office or workspace must be the principal place of business, where for example, you might meet prospective tenants.

It can be inside a house or in a detached structure on the same property, or even in an apartment you rent, provided that it is your primary residence.

Unexpected Losses

If your rental property is damaged or destroyed in a sudden event, say a fire or a flood, you may be able to deduct all or part of a loss. The same holds true for property that is stolen or vandalized.

BILL'S RULE: The SECTION 121 EXCLUSION.

President Bill Clinton signed **The Taxpayer Relief Act of 1997** into law on May 7, 1997. It provided tax relief by reducing the tax rates, while increasing the tax credits and exemptions. Now, I know we all "loved us" some Bill Clinton (even though he denied gay marriage federal protection on page 14) but really it was Speaker of the House, Newt Gingrich, (yes, Newt) who created the agenda for the reduction in capital gains tax in his <u>Contract with America</u>, which set out to balance the budget and decrease estate and capital gains tax. (Btw: President Clinton called it the "Contract <u>on</u> America"... funny Bill). Though there was considerable conflict between the Democratic President and the Republican Congress over how the budget should be written, and even a government shutdown over it, eventually a compromise was reached and this tax relief bill was made into law. It turned out to be an epic idea. In early 1998, with the economy performing better than expected, increased tax revenues helped reduce the federal budget deficit to below $25 billion. That sounds so slight compared to the expected 2015 deficit of **$564 billion**, the 2014 deficit of **$483 billion**, the 2013 deficit of **$680 billion**, and the 2012 deficit of **$1.087 billion**. Deficits are yearly. Our national debt however is combination of all our money owed. In 2018, we owed over **$20 Trillion.** Now, in the first quarter of 2024, it's over **$34 Trillion**. (sorry, no checks).

Back in 1998, Gingrich then called upon President Clinton to submit a balanced budget for 1999, which Clinton did, making it the first time the federal budget had been balanced since 1969. So, kudos to the whole bipartisan team."

Here's a quick rundown of the Tax Relief Act of 1997:

1. The top capital gains (the profit you make when you sell an investment) rate fell from 28% to 20%. The 15% bracket was lowered to 10%.

2. Starting in 1998, a $400 tax credit for each child under age 17 was introduced, which was increased to $500 in1999. (in 2018 it rose to $2,000 per child)

3. The $600,000 estate tax exemption (aka, the Death Tax) was to increase gradually to $1 million by the year 2006. (in 2017, it rose to $5.49 M per single and $10.98 M per couple)

4. Family farms and small businesses could qualify for an exemption of $1.3 million, effective 1998. (in 2017, it rose to $5.49 M)

5. Starting in 1999, the $10,000 annual gift tax exclusion was to be corrected for inflation. (in 2017 it rose to $14,000)

6. The act also provided tax relief for retirement and educations accounts.

7. Some expiring business tax provisions were extended.

Countless Americans benefited from this tax cutting and tax crediting piece of legislation. It was fiscally responsible government spending. Now, you don't have any investment accounts that you plan on selling. You don't own a farm or small business. You probably don't have any gaybies you can deduct, and you're not expecting any expensive gifts that you have to account for. Your education is already paid for and you may not have any retirement accounts to speak of. What you do have is real estate. There are definitely tax advantages to that.

Another momentary digression:

I'm sure a smarter person than I would advise you to have a more diverse investment portfolio, but I don't. There is where I am for now. I've had the thrill of making money in stocks and in commodities. It's great when you win. It feels like the easiest money you've ever made. You walk tall, feeling every bit the Wall Street Magnate you were born to be. "Why didn't I do this before?" you ask yourself. Then, in the blink of an eye, something happens and you lose your investment, and you feel lousy. Suddenly you feel small enough to play hand-ball off the curb, and you cry, "Why did I do that?"

Lesson learned: It's best to leave those kinds of investments to the professionals that study them. They have the talent and the temperament. I don't. I am not smarter than the market. Neither are you. What you and I need to do is to pay attention to the real estate market. We know a stationary, physical "brick and mortar" investment property, purchased at an opportune time, will stand the test of time and continue to earn us income over many years- and that's smart enough.

(Back to Bill's Rule)

The last part of the Tax Relief Act of 1997 is directly relevant to you, the Real Estate Investor/Investress.

Number 8. TaDaaaa! Are you with me? You'll want to learn this one. This is a real money maker- a real money <u>keeper</u>.

<u>**SECTION 121 EXCLUSION of The Tax Relief Act of 1997**</u> exempted from taxation, the profits on the sale of a personal residence, of **$250,000 for singles**, and up to **$500,000 for married couples** filing jointly. This is for <u>primary residences</u> (the house you actually live in) that you <u>lived in for at least two of the last five years</u>. (That's the criteria right there).

Say you buy a decent fixer on a nice street for $180,000. You live in it for two out of the last five years. It is your "primary residence." You sell it for $340,000. You make $160,000. That's a nice profit! Do you have to pay taxes on it according to Section 121 of TRA of 1997? No, you don't.

This is great news for home sellers and investors. This doesn't help those that flip houses, because they don't live in the house for any length of time. That's the deal. You need to <u>live</u> in it. For you the real estate investor, buy a property and make it your legal residence, while enjoying the accomplishment of adding value and equity to the house. The time will pass and you will have it on the market before you know it. You have up to five years to sell. Pick a good time to sell. Remember, "get out while the gettin's good." Take your profit and move on.

There is no limit on the number of homes you can sell and reap from this tax-free gain, but each sale must be at least two years apart. You can sell your residence this year, pocket any gain within the tax limits and buy a new residence. Two years later, you can do the same thing, again and again every two years.

You don't have to buy another home with the proceeds/profit of your sale. You could use that money to travel South America in style. You could buy an RV and drive across the country. You could purchase a Catalina 42 and sail the seven seas. You could adorn yourself with a fashionable European clothing line. You could acquire a hydrotherapy tub, steam shower and spray tanning equipment and open up a gay day spa. (You could probably retire on that alone). However suitable a name it may be, you cannot name the spa, <u>The Naked Man,</u> sorry. The queer clothier on page 70 already took that one. Well, you'll think of something.

Two more advantages:

While this tax break only applies to your primary residence, you can also use it on your rental property. (This tax act keeps giving and giving). You can turn a rental house into your primary residence, making the sale of it eligible for this significant tax savings. Another important bonus is that the actual occupancy of the home doesn't have to be sequential. The IRS lets you aggregate, or combine, your time living in the house to meet the two-year residency requirement as long as it is within 2 of the last 5 years you owned the property. For example: for the first three years you rented out the house, and then moved into it as your main home for the final two before you sold it- or you lived in it for one year, rented it out for another, and then moved back in for another year before you sold it- any combination.

Just to give you some perspective, before May 7, 1997, the only way you could avoid paying taxes on your home sale profit was to use the money to buy another, more expensive house within two years. Sellers age 55 or older had one other option. They could take a once in a lifetime tax exemption of up to $125,000 in profits. In both instances, there was tax paperwork to fill out to show that you followed all the specific rules.

One <u>disadvantage</u>:

Section 121 of the TRA of 1997 may have generated an unintended lock-in effect on houses with capital gains over the maximum exclusion amount. The home owners are "locked in" (stuck in place) if $500,0000 is the maximum exclusion amount. Sure, $500k is a lot of tax-free money, but some properties, <u>many</u> properties have increased in value far more than that. This could almost be called, "an embarrassment of riches." You've made <u>so</u> much money on your house ($500,000) that you can't sell it without taking a tax hit. This a very much a "quality problem."

Quick digression: Think of that. That's why investing in real estate creates so much wealth, so many millionaires. Your property increases in value, and you don't have to do anything but live in it (or rent it out) and take care of it. When the time is right, and tax laws benefit you, you are allowed to keep all the equity, value, cash when you sell. That's why we say, "You make money at the buy". It is the purchase price that figures your profit. The lower the <u>buy</u>, the higher the profit. Sell – Buy = Profit.

So, what needs to happen if so many people are sitting on more than $500,000 and are stuck in place? The government needs to <u>raise</u> the limits to match the increased property values. It is likely the government will increase the limits to **$500,000** for individuals and **$1000,000** for couples.

I've heard that discussed in a recent real estate meeting. If that happens, I suspect there will be a great wave of homeowners cashing out, knowing that they'll be allowed to make and <u>keep</u> so much more of their profit.

In conclusion:

Under our plan of buying low, improving, renting and then selling (using Bill's Rule) you are positioning yourself to make and keep a significant profit, <u>then</u> you go out and buy an income property for <u>cash</u>. The monthly rent on your new income property is your <u>passive income</u> (because it's not coming from earned wages) which is also your <u>disposable income</u>, which will last for as long as you own this rental property. Financial freedom is now yours! That's it! You did it! You're the man!

PROPOSITION 60, 90 & 110

Property taxes can differ from state to state. There are many tax benefits granted to people 55 or over, and to those who are disabled. For example, there are Propositions 60, 90 and 110. The state will allow you to keep the original tax basis from the house you are selling and transfer it to the house you are buying. If it's <u>within the same county, it's Prop 60</u>. If it's from <u>another participating county, it's Prop 90</u>. It's <u>Proposition 110</u> that <u>allows transfers for severely and permanently disabled property owners within the same or different county</u>. For example, say you bought a house for $100,000. Your yearly property tax is based on that amount. Five years down the road you sell it for $500,000. According to Prop 60 you need to buy a house of "equal or lesser value", $500,000 or below, but your yearly taxes are based on your previous $100,000 home. Good huh?

So, with <u>Section 121of the Tax Relief Act of 1997 you save on the Capital Gains Tax when you sell</u>, and with <u>Proposition 60, 90 & 110, you save on yearly property taxes when you buy</u>. That's a good deal, and certainly an incentive to buy low, improve, gain equity and sell for the profit, knowing that your new replacement property taxes can be based on your "old" original property (if you're 55 or over).

HAPPY ENDINGS

Another close call/lucky break from the last presidential campaign was that they conceded to continue the Section 121 Exclusion of the Tax Relief Act of 1997, what I called, "Bill's Rule." Like the Mortgage Interest Deduction, its continuance was also in question. The National Association of Realtors pressured, and massaged Congress to keep it in force. The happy ending here is that they <u>did</u>.

Repealing the Section 121 Exclusion of Tax Relief Act of 1997 would have the same damaging effect as if they repealed the Mortgage Interest Deduction: jobs, commerce and the overall economy would suffer. There would be far less incentive to invest in properties to fix and sell. Why bother?

Under our plan of buying low, improving, gaining equity, renting and/or selling, our immediate goal is to realize a healthy profit. You're counting on the profit of a sale to finance your next purchase, hopefully for <u>cash</u>.

You're working to become financially independent, if not wealthy from real estate. You want to be on F.I.R.E. – Financially Independent and Retire Early. You're not going to want to share any of your hard-earned, well-deserved profit with anyone or anything, not even with your government. This doesn't make you un-American. This makes you self- supporting. Besides, with the Section 121 Exclusion, they're not asking you to share. You just keep doing what you're doing. Uncle Sam will be fine. Don't worry about him. He'll hit you up every April.

1031 EXCHANGE

Another way to avoid paying capital gains tax on real estate profit is called the 1031 Exchange. Basically, you are exchanging the profit from the sale of one property (known as "the relinquished property") for the purchase of another one (known as "the replacement property")

The first important condition of a 1031 Exchange is that they must be of "like-kind." Like-kind refers to how a property is held and used by the Investor. It's all about your intent here. If your intention is to purchase a property as your personal home, you can't exchange the profits from its sale into purchasing another personal home. 1031 Exchanges are not for that. (It's nothing personal dear). Your intention must be to hold a property as an investment, or for use in your trade or business- be it residential/rental, commercial or industrial property- again, not personal property.

The second condition is the time limits: 45/180 days. You need to identify both properties within 45 of closing the first. 180 days from that same closing date, you have to close on the second one.

In the future, when the replacement property is sold, and is not part of another exchange, the deferred gain on the first house plus any additional gain on the second house is subject to tax, but only because that first profit helped you afford a more expensive property, so it's sale is subject to tax.

For our purposes the Section 121 Exclusion (of theTax Relief Act of 1997) is better for our plan because you get to keep all of your capital gain tax-free and accumulate it. After your house is paid off, and you're sittin' pretty, you can continue to invest in "non-personal" real estate and make tax-free capital gain using the 1031 Exchange, but again, this is after you've made some real money and you're on firm financial footing.

YOU <u>ARE</u> REAL ESTATE

Less you have any doubt as to your suitability of becoming a successful real estate buyer, seller, profiteer, man about town and bon vivant, consider this: <u>Real Estate and Gays are a perfect match</u>. They are well suited to each other. They go together like silver glitter lip-gloss and rainbow eye shadow, like black leather chaps and a worn pair of blue jeans, like stainless steel nipples clamps and a locking silicone ball gag, all kinds of real estate for all kinds of queers.

The very same words that describe real estate, describe gays, describe <u>you</u>. Think about it. Are you not: captivating and charismatic, distinct and desirous, elegant, exquisite and enchanting, impeccable, irresistible, and inviting, soothing and sophisticated, stylish and stunning?" Does that not describe <u>you</u>? Of course it does! You are all that and mooore! So, don't worry if real estate is for you. It <u>is</u> you darling!

HGTV HOTTIES

There's a whole network designed for us, the gay homebuyer. It's called <u>Homo and Gay Television</u>, or HGTV as it's commonly known. They refer to it as <u>Home and Garden Television</u> but we know better. I mean c'mon, look at these pretty boys. It's all eye candy, all the time.

Who watches more HGTV than anyone else besides our mothers? We gays! It's clear they know what they're doing when they put two young, handsome, well-built Italian men working together in close quarters and calling it <u>Cousins Undercover</u>, formerly <u>Cousins On Call</u>. Maybe the former name wasn't suggestive enough. Maybe <u>Cousins on Booty Call</u> would have been more enticing. Either way, it's evident the show's producers know their audience. A passing camera shot looking down onto broad shoulders, or across a muscular bicep, or featuring a firm, strong rear end is by no means an accidental angle. They're keeping us interested, excited- aroused even.

Their weekly line up is laced with provocative, titillatingly entitled entertainment. Take the show <u>Holmes on Homes</u> for example. It looks like, it sound like, <u>Homos on Homos</u>. You know it does. They know it too. They could've just as easily called it, <u>Mike's Makeover</u>, but that's not as spicy, not as alluuuring.

Your mother likes to watch Mike Holmes. She's quick to exclaim, "Oh I like that show! He seems like such a <u>nice</u> man." Ya Mom. You like that show because he's a masculine, mature, model of a man. Guess what? We like him too, and for the same reasons.

HGTV also has a show called, <u>All American Handyman</u> where they pit strong, toned, athletic men in a sweaty competition of construction. Occasionally, they season the show's competitive crew with a pretty yet formidable female. They don't want to be too obvious. Besides, it's interesting, compelling to watch a woman competently have her way with a few heavy-duty power tools. (Maybe that's just me).

There's also <u>Bath Crashers, </u><u>Bang for Your Buck, </u><u>Design for the Sexes, </u><u>Property Brothers</u> and <u>Man's Land</u>- and who doesn't want to live <u>there</u>?

Don't forget, <u>Bodacious Backyards</u>. Please, when have you ever heard the word, "bodacious" to describe anything but a sexy, substantially busted, voluptuous babe? The only things bodacious on HGTV are Sandra Rinomato and Egypt Sherrod who should team up and host a show of their own. They could call it, <u>The Double D Demo Duo</u>. They've got to draw those sister-loving sisters and straight-boy brothers in too.

Perhaps the most stimulating show title of them all is <u>Property Virgins</u>. There's a bounty of interested viewing voyeurs that like to watch young virgins muddle through their search for, "the right one". The deal is also conceived and consummated in <u>My First Place</u>. Maybe we just like the reminiscence of it all. I mean, who doesn't remember their first?

With salacious titles like these, I know it won't be long until they have even gayer appealing programming. What's next? <u>Garages, Gardens and Glory Holes</u>? <u>Back Door Men</u>? <u>Manhood Wood Working</u>? <u>Frat House Fixers</u>? Think of the possibilities!

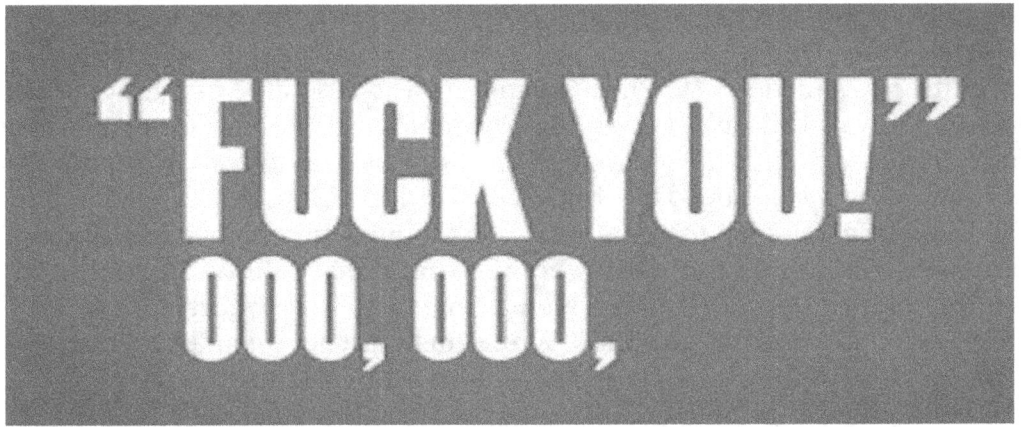

FUCK YOU MONEY

First off: I'm not just cussing to be interesting or inflammatory or crass. Though I may sound like some bog-pickin', beer-swingin', shanty-Irishman, I am not. (I'm gay) That's what it's called. Henceforth (gay!) we'll call it "F.U. Money".

Big Hugh, that stockbroker friend of mine from page 15 taught me this expression too. When he used it, I didn't know what he meant. I had never heard it before. I didn't even know there was such a thing. This sounds like a term my father would have taught me. Well, if you are lacking the mentorship, attention and instruction from your father, or maybe you weren't paying attention that day, read on.

What it is:

F.U. Money is an intense, vivid (and crude) way of saying you have sufficient money to be completely, financially independent. You are solvent. You have enough money so that if you said, "Fuck you" to an employer or to a business proposition, it wouldn't adversely affect your comfortable standard of living. You can maintain your desired lifestyle without needing employment or assistance from anyone.

Without it:

Without F.U. Money, you may be desperately bound to your job. When you're desperate to keep your job, your boss knows it. They can see it on you. They can smell it on you. They can use it against you. They can make you one frightful, frantic, nervous Nellie. Not-so-good for you.

Many of us know what it's like to live hand to mouth, paycheck to paycheck. We've felt worried, panicked, overwhelmed as we play, "the bill pay shuffle." We know losing our job would be crushing defeat. No matter how difficult bill paying is on our present income, still, it is an income that we can't do without. As a result, we say what we need to say, and do what we need to do to keep our jobs. Sometimes we have to fall on a grenade, take the heat, bite our tongues to keep our positions of employment. Sometimes we're forced to eat crow, followed by a little humble pie for dessert. It is not a meal to enjoy. It is abhorrent, detestable, downright sickening. While this may not be an everyday meal, it is not one you easily forget. Its aftertaste is long lasting ("Bitter" party of one).

With it:

With F.U. Money, you have a financial cushion. You'll give off a different scent, an air of ease and stability. You'll breathe comfortably, think clearer and feel fitter. F.U. Money gives you options; a way out, a place to go if the going gets tough and you've had enough. It allows you to confidently push back if pushed, and if that push becomes a shove, you can say, "Fuck you!" You don't have to actually curse in someone's face, although you are certainly in a position to do so. It's more of a state of being. You are confident without being self-righteous, secure without being pompous. You've reached your limit. You've taken all you're going to take. The fat lady has sung. Pigs have flown. Hell has frozen over. The floodgates have been blown open and you're looking for higher ground, but before you go...make sure you thoroughly enjoy this delicious, delectable, dynamic moment when you can finally proclaim, "Fuck you. I am done!"

As you walk away, because you have to walk away, relish in every step with the bold, assertive, dignity, and self-respect of a Pam Grier in the 1974 classic, Foxy Brown. Yaaaa. "She's brown sugar and spice, but if you don't treat her nice, she'll put you on ice." If you missed that one, or you weren't even born yet, and you're stuck for a swan song, you can always turn around to assert a slow, satisfying and savory, "Okaaaaay?" You've been saving that one for just the right occasion. Now's the time. Let her out.

How do I get some?
Unless you were born wealthy, have a large inheritance, or won the lottery, any money you have is hard earned and well deserved. That money is not extra money or passive income. It is earned and spent. If you're able to save enough over time, great! That can become your f.u. money- but will it last?

Assuming you don't like this subservient, servile, subordinate
position (and some of you s&m'rs may) you need to acquire a long term,
secure, passive income source that gives you financial security. You know
what I mean. You know what will get the job done. It's why we're here.
It's Real Estate.

Follow our plan of buying low, improving, gaining equity, renting
and/or selling, until you can buy one or two properties whose rents
pay the monthly mortgage payment, and hopefully gives you a net
spendable each month. Remember though, the plan is to be able to
make enough money to buy a property for cash, then the yearly
income is all cash flow, all passive, disposable income, all f.u. money.

Though "F.U. Money" is not a term you hear discussed in
open, professional, financial, business settings, its existence is
very real.

If you invest and protect your money through real estate, if you
follow our plan, you will have a very self-reliant, self-supportive
and financially secure life. That's a very independent position to be in.
That's the position you need to start working towards.

REVERSE MORTGAGE

This topic comes near the end of our book, because it comes at the end of our plan of buying low, improving, gaining equity, renting and/or selling and then buying more property (ultimately for cash). This is an additional income producing opportunity for you to know, one that you would do well to consider as you manage your real estate deals and plan for your financial security.

A <u>Reverse Mortgage</u> is for when you're done, when you've reached a point where you have one or more properties that are paid off or close to it. You are now a man of means, with an income that keeps you in the stylish, gay, sexy, fabulous lifestyle you are accustomed. A Reverse Mortgage is loan product; more than a loan really. It is more of an income stream that allows you to convert your property equity into cash.

As you'll recall, a HELOC, a home equity line of credit, is also a loan based on the equity in your property. A Reverse Mortgage is like that also, but the payments go in reverse. Instead of you paying the loan back to your lender each month, each month your lender pays you. (sweet!)

The loan is repaid in full when you die, sell your home, or when your home is no longer your primary residence.

This is yet another reason, another benefit to purchasing real estate. Your property pays you again, only this is not rent, tax deductions, a refinance, or even a heloc. This is a way to earn money from your real estate without having to rent it out or sell it.

You don't even have to entirely own the property to take out a Reverse Mortgage, but you should own the lion's share of it. It would be better if you owned the property entirely, because then your monthly Reverse Mortgage advances would be more. That would be ideal.

Here's the thing, you need to be at least 62 years old to take advantage of this income producing opportunity. It is not taxable, and generally does not affect your Social Security or Medicare benefits. This could bring in the extra money you need to pay off your current mortgage or supplement your retirement income or health care bills.

Whether you're a younger gay just starting out, a middle-aged chap thinking about his retirement, or a seasoned senior silver daddy looking to earn some extra money for your massages and tennis lessons at the club, this is viable income stream that you can plan for and count on.

A Reverse Mortgage is something to think about as you maneuver your real estate transactions. If you follow the plan: buy low, improve it, gain equity, rent and/or sell it to buy more properties, then you are sitting on a very real source of income in your retirement years.

If you don't buy it low enough and do the work to improve it, you're not going to realize the kind of profit needed to sell and buy another-just keep that in mind. I know every deal won't be a win fall, but you need to accumulate profit so you can buy property for cash, or you make enough money to eventually pay off your mortgage (through rents or additional sales) and own a property free and clear. That's always been our intention, only now you're learning <u>another</u> way to make money from property you own: The Reverse Mortgage.

Using a Reverse Mortgage on a property that is paid for will make <u>any</u> property an income producing property. If it's already an income producing property like a duplex, you can collect rental income and the income from the Reverse Mortgage advances (Double dip Dude).

Lastly, this could be the way to go if you want to stick it to your queer- fearing, irrational relatives who think they're going to inherit your property when you die. Little do they know that when you move on to your "great reward," <u>your</u> house will go to the Reverse Mortgage Lender. I guess you could call that another type of F.U. Money (you spiteful thing).

CONDOS

If for some reason(s) you can't follow our plan of purchasing real estate, improving it, gaining equity, renting and/or selling it until you can support yourself or buy properties for cash, you do have other options: Condos, Townhouses, Co-ops, Mobile or Manufactured Homes, and Own Your Owns. Either of these real estate holdings can give you security, and some of these, income.

Let's take Condos. We all know them. We know that Condo is short for Condominium. That's a start. A condominium is a form of home ownership in which individual units of a larger complex are sold, not rented like an apartment building. A condo complex can be renovated apartments, townhouses or even commercial warehouses. Those who purchase units in a condo, technically own everything from their walls inward, the space they live in. On the outside of their walls, all of the individual homeowners have shared ownership rights to most common areas, such as the elevators, hallways, pools and clubhouses. With a condo however, there is a noticeable lack of privacy in the common areas. The pool must be shared with every other owner (and their kids) so there'll be no skinny-dipping in the warm afternoon sun.

Then there's the upkeep: If you enjoy the satisfaction of mowing your lawn and caring for your garden and everything else- forget it. Maintenance of these areas becomes the responsibility of the Condominium Association. Every owner is part of this association and must pay monthly dues, or special assessment fees for larger maintenance problems. There is no getting out of paying these dues- unless you default on them. They are the reason why you never actually <u>own</u> this property. You are part of an Association, not an independent owner.

Many times the Association fees are higher on condominiums due to insurance and maintenance of the common elements: the pool, clubhouse, tennis courts, gay saunas and steam rooms. The last two alone could deplete its financial reserves. The final blow is that unlike the interest you pay on a mortgage, these condo and HOA dues are <u>not</u> tax deductible. For some, that's reason enough not to buy a condo or townhouse.

Condo Associations hold monthly meetings. Decisions are made which can cost all the owners money but may not equally benefit all. For example, one of your condo neighbors has fallen on hard times and has repeatedly defaulted on his dues. The board has decided to raise everyone else's dues to cover his delinquency. Is that fair? What can they do? The money has to come from somewhere, someone.

It's nearly impossible to avoid being affected by at least one condo board decision, so active participation in meetings and discussions may be more necessary than you might expect or want. If you need a monthly dose of <u>drama</u>, you can fill your prescription there.

Generally speaking, condos are easier to buy because they are less expensive than single family residences because you're not buying the land or getting the exclusivity of living on your <u>own</u> property. Conversely, condos can be harder to sell for those same reasons.

Getting the financing to buy a condo or townhouse is more difficult because lenders want to see, along with your ability to repay, the Association's financial records. They want to see a constant, consecutive, continuous current of cash being earned. This investigation is what's known as their "due diligence." They will also want to know the vacancy rate, any special assessments for repairs or upgrades, as well as any prior or pending lawsuits against the Association. They want to confirm all these facts before they risk loaning you the money to invest in this building, this HOA.

You should inspect the books too. Don't be shy about asking for them. Your Realtor can get them for you. It's standard procedure for the Association's Secretary to disclose them for review. If you're not adept at reviewing financial records, find someone who is. Don't pass that up, really. You need to have a sense of their finances before you buy into the place.

In sum: If your goal is to make this your home and live in it for many years, then condos are an affordable alternative to single family residences.

If your goal is to create a profit (net spendable) after purchasing and renting out your new condo, then your profit potential is very limited by your mortgage, and by the ever-increasing Association dues. Though condos may <u>cost</u> less than single family residences, they also <u>rent</u> for less. Your net spendable may not be worth the trouble.

Of course, if you buy your condo for cash, there's clearly more of a net-spendable, because you're not paying a mortgage, only the Association dues.

Before you even buy a condo, however affordable it may be, you should check with the Association's rental policy. Depending on the <u>Covenants, Codes and Restrictions</u> (the CC&R's) the Association may not even <u>allow</u> owners to rent out their condos. You need to know that before, not after, you write the check.

If your goal is to buy something affordable and watch it grow in value and increase in equity, ahhhh, don't hold your breath on this one. Condominiums often appreciate in value much slower than single family homes. Again, this is because you don't own any land. You only own the living space. There's the big difference. It is the <u>land</u> that really drives the appreciation.

Lastly, if you already are a well-to-do, successful, accomplished Gentlegay, who has already made their fortune, then you're already remarkable in your own right. You don't need to <u>care</u> about occasionally fluctuating condo dues or net spendables, or equity appreciation. You've already been there, lived there and left. To <u>you</u> I suggest a condo, but not just <u>any</u> condo. You don't have to go a condo-minimum, go condo-<u>maxi</u>mum. Celebrate your success!

Enjoy the uncompromising, unadulterated, unparalleled, unapologetic stately sophistication, and timeless classical grandeur of Luxury Estate Living. With fertile, manicured, garden landscaped architecture, sweeping panoramic vistas and strong, handsome, compliant concierge service personnel at your command, you will live like a Prince, a King, a Queeeen!

TOWNHOUSES

Historically a "Townhouse" was the name used to refer to the city residence of a member of the wealthy and privileged noble class of society. From the 18th century landowners and their servants would move to their city townhouses during the social season, when major balls and social galas (and gay pride parades) took place. When the season ended, they would pack up their rich fabulous selves and return to their country home, where they enjoyed lavish luxury living for the rest of the year.

Many people consider condos and townhouses as the same type of housing. That is not so. Repeat after me, "A townhouse is not a condo." "........ ." Very good.

Townhouses are sometimes called "row houses" because they're usually identical properties in a row, with one or both sides sharing common walls, depending on where they are in the row. They can be built as single or multi-storied structures. They can be grouped together as single family units, as duplexes or triplexes, or they can be a part of a huge complex.

Typically, ownership of townhouses comes with the little patch of land that the house is actually <u>on</u>. That's called "fee simple" (for you terminology nerds) That simply means that you not only own your <u>unit</u>, but the ground <u>below</u> it. Condo ownership does <u>not</u> come with any land. That's the distinct difference between the two- the land.

Townhouse Association dues are typically lower than Condo dues because they cover fewer things. The Association may cover roof repair and replacement, exterior maintenance and common area maintenance. Like a condo, it is a very low maintenance lifestyle, which is part of their appeal, but it doesn't come cheap. Also like a condo, there are the Association restrictions, fees and politics to deal with.

Both condominiums and townhouses are generally cheaper than single family homes, <u>but</u> we're here to do <u>more</u> than just buy a property and keep up the payments. Buy a property where your financial future is not subject to increasing monthly dues or Association politics and power.

We have a <u>plan</u> here. We are here to invest, repair, gain equity, rent for the income and/or sell for the profit, until we can eventually buy one or more properties for <u>cash</u>. We can live off the rents or have the security of living in a property that is mortgage free. In that course, we become financially independent and self-sufficient.

If you really want the opportunity to improve your economic outlook and increase your financial worth, don't buy a Townhouse. The HOA dues and lack of exclusivity will keep the property's value and desirability down, as compared to a single-family residence.

Condos and Townhouses won't help you achieve your goal of financial freedom, more likely they will <u>rob</u> you of it. You can pick one up after you've made your first million, until then, stick with the plan.

CO-OPS/STOCK COOPERATIVES

I'm going to throw <u>Stock Cooperatives/Co-ops</u> into the mix here. They're not very common in my area, but they may be in yours. If someone tries to sell you one, run away Fay. They're not for you- not if you're just beginning- not if you hope to make any money in real estate investing.

As with a condo or townhouse, you can buy a Co-op <u>after</u> you've become successful, when you want or need more rigid, formal CC&R's. For now, you need the flexibility that comes from following your <u>own</u> covenants, codes and restrictions.

A Stock Cooperative/Co-op is a multi-unit apartment building where each resident has an interest, a share in the entire building. Co-op owners are often called "shareholders", because they own shares as members of the corporation that owns the co-op. The larger the unit, the more shares they own.

These shareholders aren't even called "owners." They are referred to as "tenants." They don't actually own their particular unit. They have a lease enabling them to occupy it.

If you're <u>not</u> going to own, then what's the point? Our goal is to <u>own</u> not rent, not to be tenants, not to be shareholders, not to be members, not to be valued by the size of our units. We want to own undeniably, indisputably, unconditionally. We're not interested in their <u>units</u> or their <u>members</u>. Let's keep it professional here.

There's also an Association to deal with. It's comprised of all of the Shareholders combined, or by an elected Board of Directors. The Association makes management and financial decisions, either through voting at regularly scheduled meetings or by the Board of Directors that handle the day-to-day operations.

These folks also have the power to approve or disapprove of prospective Buyers. They can also terminate membership and evict residents who violate any part of the occupancy agreement. (Can you imagine having to audition for that group? Bring your tap shoes honey) I suppose if they reject your gay, sexy, fabulous self, you can always throw a tizzy-fit and shrill "Homo Haterrrrr!"

Regarding financing: In recent years, co-op financing has been freely available and is referred to as "share loan financing." You're technically buying shares of a corporation. The Lender usually wants to affirm that the building has at least a 50% occupancy rate.

If a Buyer is unable to get the entire amount needed to close the deal, the Seller "takes back" or loans money to the buyer with interest. The Buyer signs a promissory note, and the Seller retains a share of his ownership in the building. This is a very confusing and convoluted way to buy real estate. The Seller is holding the paper, carrying a note, and would own a portion of your share of the property, of the corporation.

Whether it's a condo, co-op or townhouse, the option of having the Seller "carry the note," "hold the paper," "take back" the loan is almost never a good one. That's rarely an option you should choose. Remember Cruella from page 141?

Also, in a co-op, you can forget about buying one to make it a rental. They're having none of that there. Co-op buyers buy to live-in, not rent-out their units. They don't want any troublesome, transitory tenants, or lazy, lackadaisical, landlords sharing their living space, even if it's only a passing glance in the lobby, or God forbid, a quick ride share in the elevator. Actually, I don't blame them. They just want to control their environment and maintain the quality and value of their building. Who can find fault with that?

Just don't put any "Irish Need Not Apply" signs in the window and we're good. Thank you, or, "Go raibh maith agot." (pronounced, guh rev mah ah- gwiv) in Gaelic (pronounced Gay-lick). Yes, I went there.

MOBILE AND MANUFACTURED HOMES

The early images of mobile homes bring to mind the rickety, hand-built, cabin trailers that became popular during The Great Depression era, as gypsies, tramps and thieves, (nod to Ms. Bono) travelled from town to town searching for work. However, beginning in the 1950s, these types of homes started to become a more functioning and fashionable form of housing, designed to be set up and left in locations for long periods of time, or even permanently installed with a masonry foundation. These little units were only about eight feet wide, or less. In 1956, the 10-foot wide trailer was introduced, along with its newer, cooler, hipper term "Mobile Home." These larger, wider units ("ten-wide", and later, "twelve-wide") usually required the services of a professional trucking company and often a special moving permit from a state highway department.

During the late 1960s and early 70s, mobile homes were made even longer and wider, making the mobility of the units more difficult. Today, when a mobile home is moved to a location, it is usually kept there- permanently.

The term "Mobile Home" was given to units constructed before June 1976. Homes constructed after June 1976 are almost always known as "Manufactured Homes,"

If you want to buy either a mobile or manufactured home, it's important to know your financing options.

There is a difference in how mobile homes and manufactured homes are financed. Mobile homes that are permanently installed on owned land (usually mobile home parks) are rarely mortgageable, whereas FHA approved manufactured homes <u>are</u> mortgageable.

Most banks won't finance mobile homes when there is no land, or "lot" included in the loan. (As with condos, there's no land to drive the value) There are some companies that specialize in mobile home financing. They finance and refinance mobile homes in parks.

The restrictions on loans involving manufactured homes require that the unit be brand new and come with its own (relatively small) lot. It must then be sold to the new occupant as a package deal. (As with a townhouse, it sits on its own land). The biggest problem with this program is that once the unit has been lived in, any new buyer that comes along, wouldn't be able to qualify for that same type of loan because it is no longer new. It's been lived in. This requirement makes it difficult for a seller to sell, and the would-be buyer to buy.

There is also the tendency for both the mobile and manufactured homes to depreciate in value when resold. This makes using them as collateral for loans much riskier than traditional home loans. If you were to find mobile or manufactured home financing, the terms and conditions would be similar to financing a car. The interest would be higher and the term shorter, say, 5 years to pay it back.

Regarding taxes: in some states, mobile homes have been taxed as personal property if the wheels remain attached, but if it is stationary, with no wheels, it is taxed as real estate.

If you don't own the land that your mobile/manufactured home sits on, then you have to pay space rent each month. That space rent, like a condo or townhouse association fee, is <u>not</u> tax-deductible.

In short, you may not be able to get a decent loan to buy it. If you are able to buy it, it doesn't retain its value over time. You pay rent for the land it sits on. That rent is subject to increase and is <u>not</u> tax deductible.

Mobile or manufactured homes would fit in at the end of our plan, after you've purchased your income property and/or home for cash, and you have a net spendable, disposable income coming in each month.

If you think you can include these in your plan to buy, fix, hold and sell, think again. You can't. They do not appreciate in value. They're not single-family homes or income properties. <u>Those</u> are the properties that make our plan work, that make money, big money, if worked attentively and intelligently.

If already have your house paid off, maybe have an additional income property or two, then buying a mobile or manufactured home is something to consider. I know. I have two mobile homes (that family members occupy). If you buy one for cash, you wouldn't have a mortgage payment. Your only monthly fee would be the lot fee, which is usually reasonable- and of course taxes and insurance - which are usually low on these mobile/"manny" houses. Your monthly nut would be quite easy to chew. If you were to rent out the unit, the tenant would pay those bills anyway. That's why they're there.

As with any rental, you need to figure out how much you can make on the cost of the unit, the financial return on your investment. You're not buying it for the profit potential when you sell this mobile home. You already know they don't hold their value. You're buying it for the rent, the return, the income, the interest on your investment. Remember Cap Rate from page 109? That applies here too. What would be the Cap Rate for a Mobile home you purchase for $30,000? You rent it out for $1000 a month. You pay $300 for space rent and $100 a month goes to taxes and insurance. (You clear $600 x 12 = $7200 / $30,000). It would be 24%. You would make 24% a year on your $30,000 investment. If you were buying it for cash, that's a great return on your money. Even if you were to finance it at say, 5%: 24% made minus 5% paid is <u>19%.</u> That's still an excellent interest rate on your investment.

Lastly, this mobile/manny option is also an easier way to buy a home with no muss, no fuss, no hard work or tenants- just a humble home to hang your hat. They're even more affordable if you're 55 years or older. There are senior parks that use a sliding income scale to determine their space rents. That's a nice opportunity for some of you senior gay gents. That's also something to plan for, for some of you mid-career men.

While mobile/manufactured homes aren't going to make you rich, they are an affordable way to go, if you just want to own a simple, inexpensive place to live.

So live in it- don't live in it- rent it out- don't rent it out- enjoy long secluded stays or brief boy-toy trysts. The options are yours because you <u>own</u> it.

www.shutterstock.com · 84062407

OWN YOUR OWNS

Own Your Owns are a form of real estate ownership that pre-dates the condominium form of ownership. They are usually 2 or 3 stories, typically in 8-12 unit buildings, tucked between newer and sometimes taller buildings. Own Your Owns were mostly built in the 1950's. Many people find these types of units appealing because of their mid-century characteristics, with older tiled bathrooms, hardwood floors, and more intimate settings. I find them appealing because of their price. They are less expensive than condos, and a lot easier to manage. I own and manage six of them.

The challenge with buying OYO's is the financing. Not all lenders write OYO loans, and the ones that do, usually want you to have 20% down, and be an owner occupier.

One major reason why they are less expensive than condos is- parking. Usually there isn't enough, if any at all. For that reason, they cost <u>less</u> than a condo on the same street. If you don't mind that the building only has street parking, you can pick up a nice OYO for significantly less than a neighboring condo. Some people, some perspective tenants, may not need or care about parking. It is the <u>unit</u> that they're going to call home, that interests them the most. That's the part you control. Whether there is parking or not is <u>out</u> of your control. Your job is to provide a nice, comfortable and clean unit to rent. Such a place will earn you a favorable, faithful tenant.

If your OYO building, "Goes Condo," is converted to condominiums, the value of the unit dramatically increases, and the owner/investor/you make a significant profit. That's great, but that potential isn't the <u>only</u> reason to invest in an OYO.

There is the <u>income potential</u> and <u>cap rate</u> that makes it immediately profitable. There is also the satisfaction of knowing that your money is secured by a physical investment.

Purchasing an Own Your Own to live in would be comparable to purchasing a mobile home to live in, if you just want a place to own, one that you hold Title to. At the very least, it would accomplish the goal of owning. I'm thinking more in terms of an OYO being an investment to earn you an <u>income</u>. Even though it costs less than a condo, often the rental income can be nearly the same, therefore the return on your investment can be as good, if not better. Remember Cap Rate from pg 109? Also, the monthly HOA fees are next to nothing, because there's usually nothing there to maintain and cost the owner extra money.

Say you followed the plan. You bought and sold a couple of houses. You made some money, paid off your residence, maybe have a duplex making you a decent income. You feel comfortable enough to invest in something else. Why have your money sitting in the bank doing nothing- making nothing. Put it in a profitable, income producing property. It will beat any interest a bank will pay you.

In an OYO building, you're usually not dealing with HOA politics and power, just people who want a low-key property with a good return. As OYOs are smaller buildings with less amenities, the monthly fees are less. They pay for the property management company to maintain the books and keep up the place.

We know that finding financing to purchase an OYO can be challenging. The same may be true when you go to sell it. You're going to need a buyer who is ready with a good 20% down. That may not be so easy to do. Those units that <u>do</u> sell are often All-Cash purchases, or Seller Financing deals, where the seller, "holds the paper" or "carries the loan" as discussed on page 139. If you are the seller of an OYO, this may be an option for you. You may <u>have</u> to carry some of the paper if you need to sell that little money maker of yours. Depending on the terms you set, it may still provide you a decent income - for a few years anyway.

Remember, Own your Owns aren't frilly and fabulous. There are no pools, tennis courts, hot tubs, gyms, saunas, yoga or Pilates studios, but, you're not there for that. Own Your Owns are protected, prolonged, profitable investment properties that will earn a significant interest on your money. You'll have to find somewhere else and be frilly and fabulous...as if <u>that's</u> ever a problem.

LAND TO ROAM

Sometimes you have an itch that you've got to scratch. It keeps bothering you and you want to scratch the darn thing, even though you know you shouldn't. You become distracted by the itch and think that once you scratch it you'll feel better. This can be the case in buying real estate as well.

You've been itching to buy some property. You want to buy something, anything, just to get it and feel better about not having any. You're not quite ready to buy an income producing property, never mind a condo, small house or mobile home. It bothers you, maybe dents your dignity a bit, knowing that you can't fulfill that goal, especially when you see your friends and family buying property. <u>Now</u> that little itch has turned into a full-scale dermatological disease that needs immediate treatment! You start to change your thinking. You <u>start</u> thinking that homoownership is not for everyone, not for people like you (read "gay") so you slowly modify your goal.

There <u>is</u> that parcel of land that you saw advertised in the back of the local paper. It's only about 50 miles outside of town, along that old dirt county road that no one travels. It's not very large, seemingly worthless, still you consider it for a while.

"Hmmm", you think to yourself, "True, it is remote, desolate, unused, but hey it's also quiet. I like quiet." You consider its possibilities. "I <u>could</u> put a tent on the land and camp there, or maybe even a small trailer. It could be like my home away from home, my vacation house, my escape, my retreat, my desert oasis."

If nothing else, you can <u>consider</u> yourself a property owner. Think of the bragging rights! Depending on who you're talking to, your 2500 sq. ft. mosquito-infested, weed-packed piece of prairie land, or your puny, parched plot of <u>Death Valley</u>, can suddenly become a breath-taking, plush, lush, sprawling kingdom- a veritable picturesque, pastoral, scenic wonderland! Who's going to know otherwise?

No one's going to know that <u>really</u> you've been too busy trying to make a living to put any of that Boy Scout training to use on your postage stamp of a property. No one's going to know about the letters and bills you've been getting from the County for weed abatement, trash and abandoned car removal, not to mention the taxes you have pay on it every year. Don't waste your time and energy on these undesirable lots. Sure, they make for an additional asset, but really they're just a pain <u>in</u> it. I know. I have two of them.

It's almost a running joke with seasoned real estate investors. After years of wasted time and money, they're always happy to unload their lots on to some inexperienced, speculating patsy like they used to be. So, spare yourself that rite of passage. Wait for and work for something of present or potential value.

Those lots, those parcels that <u>do</u> have value aren't going to be cheap, unless you get lucky, or have some insider, pre-development info of that area. Land on street corners, next to gas stations, near stores or businesses are all worthy of purchasing. Remember, "Under all is the land." A well-located lot can become anything: a barbershop, a bakery, a Sears or a CVS. If nothing else, an empty lot can easily be used as an income-producing parking lot. Why not?

Of course, any land next to an oil drill is top on the list. Maybe one day when you're shooting at some food, up through the ground will come some bubblin' crude. Oil that is, black gold, Texas tea (see page 64)

IN CLOSING

If you really want to improve your future, make real estate investing part of your present. Follow the plan of buying low, improving, gaining equity, renting and selling until you accumulate enough money to buy (and/or pay off) a property with cash.

A mortgage free rental property can provide you enough income to support yourself. It doesn't have to be a block of houses. One income property can do the job.

When you buy a property for cash, all of the monthly rental income is Cash Flow, Passive Income, Disposable Income. It can provide you a lifetime of self-reliance and financial security.

That's it! Financial freedom is yours! You will never again have to clock in, sign in, or report in, to be your boss's bitch. You are your own bitch. As they Dragarrattis would say, when you are a B.I.T.C.H. you are a Being In Total Control of Herself. (You go gurl)

Now, start preparing, saving, and paying attention to potential properties. Keep an open mind as to when, where and what you want to buy.

One last time, "Buy real estate, take care of it, and it will take care of you." You can do it. You want to do it. You're willing to work-it. Great!

Let's all work-it. Let's all work to increase our physical presence and improve our financial prominence. Real estate investing is a workable way and a profitable path to take. Let's leave our footprints all over it.

www.ingramcontent.com/pod-product-compliance
Lightning Source LLC
Chambersburg PA
CBHW081309170526
45166CB00011B/3461